the Lord is
my strength

the Lord is my strength

PRAYING THE PSALMS

DAY BY DAY

Eric Kampmann

PHOTOGRAPHS by ERIC, PETER, & ARTHUR KAMPMANN

**BEAUFORT
BOOKS**

NEW YORK, NY

For inquiries about volume orders, please contact:
Beaufort Books
27 West 20th Street, Suite 1102
New York, NY 10011
sales@beaufortbooks.com

Published in the United States by Beaufort Books www.beaufortbooks.com
Distributed by Midpoint Trade Books, a division of Independent Book Publishers
www.midpointtrade.com
www.ipgbook.com

Book design by Mark Karis

Library of Congress Data on file

ISBN 9780825309267

Printed in The United States

This Book Is Dedicated with Love

to

My wife, Anne

My sons, Alex, Peter, and Arthur

And my daughter, Elizabeth

And Nehemiah, who was the governor, and Ezra the priest and scribe, and the Levites who taught the people said to all the people, "This day is holy to the LORD your God; do not mourn or weep." For all the people wept as they heard the words of the Law. Then he said to them, "Go your way. Eat the fat and drink sweet wine and send portions to anyone who has nothing ready, for this day is holy to our Lord. And do not be grieved, for the joy of the LORD is your strength."

—NEHEMIAH 8:9-10

THREE THREADS

I would like to think of *The Lord Is My Strength* as an intertwining of three distinct threads that have shaped my life.

The first thread is my abiding love for mountains. This began with summer trips to the White Mountains in New Hampshire. That experience led to a love of hiking that in turn led to my first prolonged journey on the Appalachian Trail beginning in 1967. Many of the pictures in this book reflect some of the beauty, mystery, and wonder I have experienced while walking in the hills and valleys of "the great globe itself."

The second thread developed as a result of the first. At some point I picked up a camera to carry along with me to record some of what I saw and experienced.

The third thread came later in life. Like many of my generation, I put my Christian heritage aside to pursue the "cares of the world and the deceitfulness of riches and the desires for other things." (Mark 4:19) But that all came to a dramatic end in 1989. Soon enough I began the journey of a new life by pursuing Jesus Christ to "know him and to make him known." It is this life-giving thread that began to show me that I am not my own strength; nor is anyone else either. God is our strength day in and day out if we will only let him be. This realization is what ties the three threads into a celebration of God's presence and purpose for each one of us.

BLESSED IS THE MAN WHO WALKS NOT IN THE COUNSEL OF THE WICKED, NOR STANDS IN THE WAY OF SINNERS, NOR SITS IN THE SEAT OF SCOFFERS; BUT HIS DELIGHT IS IN THE LAW OF THE LORD, AND ON HIS LAW HE MEDITATES DAY AND NIGHT. *—Psalm 1:1–2*

BLESSED IS THE MAN

If we take our direction from the "counsel of the wicked" we are surely out of sorts with God. Righteousness means right with God where God is first in our lives in all things, not just some things. The truth is God calls us to be the "congregation of the righteous."

See also: Psalm 1:5–6, 1 John 3:4–7

WHY DO THE NATIONS RAGE AND THE PEOPLES PLOT IN VAIN? THE KINGS OF THE EARTH SET THEMSELVES, AND THE RULERS TAKE COUNSEL TOGETHER, AGAINST THE LORD AND AGAINST HIS ANOINTED, SAYING, "LET US BURST THEIR BONDS APART AND CAST AWAY THEIR CORDS FROM US." —*Psalm 2:1–3*

THE REVOLT AGAINST GOD

Here is the simple truth: We scheme, plot, and conspire, thinking we will never be seen or caught, but deep down we know that God knows every secret we clutch on to. We are foolish for believing God does not see the fullness of who we are. Could Adam and Eve hide from God? Can we?

See also: John 2:25; Matthew 24:6–8

BUT YOU, O LORD, ARE A SHIELD ABOUT ME, MY GLORY, AND THE LIFTER OF MY HEAD. I CRIED ALOUD TO THE LORD, AND HE ANSWERED ME FROM HIS HOLY HILL. —*Psalm 3:3–4*

I CRIED OUT TO THE LORD

When life is sweet, it is tempting to think this is the life God intended for us. But if and when storms break, are we ready? The psalmist says "the Lord sustained me." It is easy to be a "prayer agnostic" when times are good, but what is our position if troubles do arrive?

See also: Psalm 3:5

ANSWER ME WHEN I CALL, O GOD OF MY RIGHTEOUSNESS! YOU HAVE GIVEN ME RELIEF WHEN I WAS IN DISTRESS. BE GRACIOUS TO ME AND HEAR MY PRAYER! —*Psalm 4:1*

HEAR MY PRAYER

When I finally gave up insisting that I still had the strength to plow through the muck and the mire of my life, I prayed to God for help because I was a desperate man. But God foiled my doubt and skepticism. God answered my prayer showing me that He is near and He is gracious.

See also: Zechariah 1:13

BUT I, THROUGH THE ABUNDANCE OF YOUR STEADFAST LOVE, WILL ENTER YOUR HOUSE. I WILL BOW DOWN TOWARD YOUR HOLY TEMPLE IN THE FEAR OF YOU. —*Psalm 5:7*

GOD'S ABUNDANT LOVE

When we juxtapose this verse with what comes earlier in the psalm we realize that the writer's righteousness grows out of his "steadfast" faith in the Lord: "O Lord, in the morning you hear my voice; in the morning I prepare a sacrifice for you and watch."

See also: Job 28:28

LEAD ME, O LORD, IN YOUR RIGHTEOUSNESS BECAUSE OF MY ENEMIES; MAKE YOUR WAY STRAIGHT BEFORE ME. —*Psalm 5:8*

LEAD ME, O LORD

The public evidence would have suggested Job was guilty of some crime against God, but his confidence rests in the full story of his integrity that will be revealed in the end: "Let me be weighed in a just balance, and let God know my integrity."

See also: Proverbs 10:9

BE GRACIOUS TO ME, O LORD, FOR I AM LANGUISHING; HEAL ME, O LORD, FOR MY BONES ARE TROUBLED. —*Psalm 6:2*

HEAL ME, O LORD

If we assume this life is it, then we better stay young because this miracle we call the human body is ultimately flesh and blood and is subject to relentless time. The best reason to pray for a long life is to use the time we have to lavishly honor God and extend His Kingdom.

See also: Mark 2:17

MY SHIELD IS WITH GOD, WHO SAVES THE UPRIGHT IN HEART. —*Psalm 7:10*

GOD MY SHIELD

Do we need protection? Do we need a shield? Actually, no matter what we might think, we need protection every minute of every day. And our protection is to "love the Lord with all your heart, strength, soul and mind." True goodness flows from just that.

See also: Psalm 55:17

I WILL GIVE TO THE LORD THE THANKS DUE TO HIS RIGHTEOUSNESS, AND I WILL SING PRAISE TO THE NAME OF THE LORD, THE MOST HIGH. —*Psalm 7:17*

I WILL SING PRAISE

How can we know what righteousness is? I spent too much time believing the best was defined by the various "bests" nearby: the best school, the best team, the best company. But that's not it. There is something far better: we have in Jesus the perfect picture of what righteousness is.

See also: Hebrews 2:12

WHEN I LOOK AT YOUR HEAVENS, THE WORK OF YOUR FINGERS, THE MOON
AND THE STARS, WHICH YOU HAVE SET IN PLACE, WHAT IS MAN THAT YOU
ARE MINDFUL OF HIM, AND THE SON OF MAN THAT YOU CARE FOR HIM?

—Psalm 8:3–4

WHAT IS MAN?

"What is man?" asks the psalmist. He answers, "you made him a little lower than
the heavenly beings and crowned him with glory and honor." But when we do not
have a genuine connection to God, the pursuit of goodness, honor, and truth will
be shredded by our darker drives within.

See also: John 8:44

I WILL GIVE THANKS TO THE LORD WITH MY WHOLE HEART; I WILL RECOUNT ALL OF YOUR WONDERFUL DEEDS. I WILL BE GLAD AND EXULT IN YOU; I WILL SING PRAISE TO YOUR NAME, O MOST HIGH. —*Psalm 9:1–2*

I WILL GIVE THANKS

In a scene in *Hamlet*, King Claudius falls to his knees to pray but no words issue forth. His guilt has overcome his need for forgiveness. Unlike King David who confesses, Claudius' guilt is a barrier to a "whole heart." He arises, not cleansed of his sins, but entrapped by them.

See also: Psalm 51:1–5

BUT THE LORD SITS ENTHRONED FOREVER; HE HAS ESTABLISHED HIS THRONE FOR JUSTICE, AND HE JUDGES THE WORLD WITH RIGHTEOUSNESS; HE JUDGES THE PEOPLES WITH UPRIGHTNESS. —*Psalm 9:7–8*

ENTHRONED FOREVER

When political leaders substitute God's righteous throne with their own new and improved version, havoc and suffering will follow. The wars of the last century were built on assumptions of technological invention and scientific genius, resulting in more killing, not less.

See also: 2 Samuel 7:12

ARISE, O LORD! LET NOT MAN PREVAIL; LET THE NATIONS BE JUDGED BEFORE YOU! PUT THEM IN FEAR, O LORD! LET THE NATIONS KNOW THAT THEY ARE BUT MEN! —*Psalm 9:19–20*

LORD, PROTECT ME

The psalmist states that there is no justice, no safety, no goodness without our "fearing" the Lord. We have sufficient evidence that when men rule as "Masters of the Universe," then those who are ruled are subject to the untender mercies of their masters.

See also: Psalm 110:10

WHY, O LORD, DO YOU STAND FAR AWAY? WHY DO YOU HIDE YOURSELF IN TIMES OF TROUBLE? —*Psalm 10:1*

DO NOT HIDE, O LORD

Sometimes things get so bad, so hopeless that we come to believe that we have been abandoned with no hope for rescue. The wicked prosper, the weak are abused, and injustice pollutes the air. This describes the condition of the very world Jesus came to rescue.

See also: 2 Timothy 4:18

IN THE PRIDE OF HIS FACE THE WICKED DOES NOT SEEK HIM; ALL HIS THOUGHTS ARE, "THERE IS NO GOD." —*Psalm 10:4*

THE THOUGHTS OF THE WICKED

This verse gives us the crucial link between evil and the belief that "There is no God." The Russian novelist Dostoevsky prophetically said that if God does not exist all things are possible. When we disconnect from God, endless levels of depravity will grow and flourish.

See also: Genesis 6:5–6

SAVE, O LORD, FOR THE GODLY ONE IS GONE; FOR THE FAITHFUL HAVE VANISHED FROM AMONG THE CHILDREN OF MAN. —*Psalm 12:1*

THE FAITHFUL HAVE VANISHED

Have you ever been lost? Have you ever been in a place where all the comforts and diversions of civilization vanish? I suspect there are many more who have experienced abandonment than we realize. What would it be like if the familiar world of place and people suddenly was gone?

See also: Deuteronomy 31:18

THE WORDS OF THE LORD ARE PURE WORDS, LIKE SILVER REFINED IN A FURNACE ON THE GROUND, PURIFIED SEVEN TIMES. *—Psalm 12:6*

THE WORD OF GOD

The psalmist says the "words of the Lord are pure words" but then contrasts the purity and righteous of God's awesome holiness with the condition of man on earth: "On every side the wicked prowl, as vileness is exalted among the children of man."

See also: Psalm 12:8, John 1:1–2

HOW LONG, O LORD? WILL YOU FORGET ME FOREVER? HOW LONG WILL YOU HIDE YOUR FACE FROM ME? HOW LONG MUST I TAKE COUNSEL IN MY SOUL AND HAVE SORROW IN MY HEART ALL THE DAY? HOW LONG SHALL MY ENEMY BE EXALTED OVER ME? —*Psalm 13:1–2*

HOW LONG, O LORD?

What does "despair" look like? Despair has no bright colors. The world all around is painted in grays and black. Night has come and love has vanished. Without the hope that comes from a gracious God, we live as heirs of Cain. We are doomed to be "restless wanderers of the earth."

See also: Psalm 88:1–18, Genesis 4:13–16

I WILL SING TO THE LORD, BECAUSE HE HAS DEALT BOUNTIFULLY WITH ME.

—Psalm 13:6

I WILL SING TO THE LORD

The origin of music can be traced to the origins of the universe itself because song itself reflects the harmony of God's design behind all of creation. Song is our response to the recognition that "The heavens declare the glory of God..."

THE FOOL SAYS IN HIS HEART, "THERE IS NO GOD." THEY ARE CORRUPT, THEY DO ABOMINABLE DEEDS; THERE IS NONE WHO DOES GOOD.

—Psalm 14:1

THE FOOL

When the fool denies God, soon enough his behavior will change. His growing freedom from God will lead to dangerous choices; this course he has set will create trouble for himself and for others. And this seed of evil may grow to where "there is none who does good, not even one."

See also: Psalm 14:3, Isaiah 19:13

THE LORD LOOKS DOWN FROM HEAVEN ON THE CHILDREN OF MAN, TO SEE IF THERE ARE ANY WHO UNDERSTAND, WHO SEEK AFTER GOD. THEY HAVE ALL TURNED ASIDE; TOGETHER THEY HAVE BECOME CORRUPT; THERE IS NONE WHO DOES GOOD, NOT EVEN ONE. —*Psalm 14:2–3*

NOT EVEN ONE

Man without God is a ship without a compass; sooner or later it will encounter disaster. Without a strong belief in God, we randomly rummage around for answers that are not answers. Without God, we have no equilibrium; we "turn aside" to wander away toward a darker unknown.

See also: Jonah 1:1–17

O LORD, WHO SHALL SOJOURN IN YOUR TENT? WHO SHALL DWELL ON YOUR HOLY HILL? —*Psalm 15:1*

THE SOJOURNER

Who will find a home with the Lord? He answers: He who is is blameless and who does what is right; he who speaks truth, does not slander, and is faithful to his friend. Most important, he who honors those who fear the Lord. It is such as these who find rest in the Lord.

See also: Job 1:8

PRESERVE ME, O GOD, FOR IN YOU I TAKE REFUGE. I SAY TO THE LORD, "YOU ARE MY LORD; I HAVE NO GOOD APART FROM YOU." —*Psalm 16:1–2*

IN YOU I TAKE REFUGE

David knows that God comes first; he looks out at the world and finds sorrow and distress where many run after strange gods. David is not confused. There is only one God and he is the God David is serving. He says, "I have no good apart from you."

See also: Isaiah 42:5–9

I BLESS THE LORD WHO GIVES ME COUNSEL; IN THE NIGHT ALSO MY HEART INSTRUCTS ME. I HAVE SET THE LORD ALWAYS BEFORE ME; BECAUSE HE IS AT MY RIGHT HAND, I SHALL NOT BE SHAKEN. —*Psalm 16:7–8*

THE LORD INSTRUCTS MY HEART

In Athens, Paul identifies Jesus as the "Unknown God" the Athenians have been worshipping. Then, he says they should "feel their way toward him and find him. Yet, he is actually not far from each one of us" reinforcing what the psalmist says: "God is at my right hand."

See also: Acts 17:16–34

YOU MAKE KNOWN TO ME THE PATH OF LIFE; IN YOUR PRESENCE THERE IS FULLNESS OF JOY; AT YOUR RIGHT HAND ARE PLEASURES FOREVERMORE.

—*Psalm 16:11*

THE PATH OF LIFE

When we walk away from God, we may think we have discovered the way to the "good life," but soon enough we realize we have followed the same path walked by the prodigal son. What will it take to get back to the path of genuine salvation?

See also: Luke: 11–32

I CALL UPON YOU, FOR YOU WILL ANSWER ME, O GOD; INCLINE YOUR EAR TO ME; HEAR MY WORDS. —*Psalm 17:6*

HEAR MY PRAYER

Long ago, I found that I had engineered my life into a very bad and dangerous place. One day, I called to God for help. Two weeks later, God answered in an unexpected way: "BUY A BIBLE" is what I heard. It made no sense to me, but I did just that, and that step has changed everything.

See also: Act 26:19

I LOVE YOU, O LORD, MY STRENGTH. THE LORD IS MY ROCK AND MY FORTRESS AND MY DELIVERER, MY GOD, MY ROCK, IN WHOM I TAKE REFUGE, MY SHIELD, AND THE HORN OF MY SALVATION, MY STRONGHOLD.

—Psalm 18:1–2

I LOVE YOU, LORD

David depends completely on God. He calls God his fortress, his deliverer, his rock, his refuge, his shield and his stronghold. David's strength is his steadfast trust in God. The Lord is his strength.

See also: Psalm 28:7

I CALL UPON THE LORD, WHO IS WORTHY TO BE PRAISED, AND I AM SAVED FROM MY ENEMIES. —*Psalm 18:3*

I CALL UPON THE LORD

David's back is against the wall. He says, "The cords of death encompassed me; the torrents of destruction assailed me." David cannot save himself, and he knows it. In utter desperation, he calls out to God and God answers him. God is his salvation.

See also: Psalm 18:4–20

THIS GOD—HIS WAY IS PERFECT; THE WORD OF THE LORD PROVES TRUE; HE IS A SHIELD FOR ALL THOSE WHO TAKE REFUGE IN HIM. —*Psalm 18:30*

HIS WAY IS PERFECT

From the Song of Moses: "For I proclaim the name of the Lord; ascribe greatness to our God! The Rock, his work is perfect, for all his ways are justice. A God of faithfulness and without iniquity, just and upright is he."

See also: Deuteronomy 32:3–4

THE HEAVENS DECLARE THE GLORY OF GOD, AND THE SKY ABOVE PROCLAIMS HIS HANDIWORK. DAY TO DAY POURS OUT SPEECH, AND NIGHT TO NIGHT REVEALS KNOWLEDGE. THERE IS NO SPEECH, NOR ARE THERE WORDS, WHOSE VOICE IS NOT HEARD. —*Psalm 19:1–3*

THE GLORY OF GOD

Can our words capture the splendor and mystery of the universe? The stars, the sun, the moon declare the "glory of God." And the beauty of it all is there right before us, not as words or speech or sound, but as a vast canvas that displays the wonder of God's creation itself.

See also: Romans 1:18–23

THE LAW OF THE LORD IS PERFECT, REVIVING THE SOUL... —*Psalm 19:7A*

THE LAW OF THE LORD

The greatest law of the Lord is straightforward: Love the Lord your God with your whole heart, soul, strength, and mind. Everything good flows from putting God above everything else, including the people and things we love very dearly. Yet what seems simple, proves hard for many.

See also: Mark 12:28–31

...THE TESTIMONY OF THE LORD IS SURE, MAKING WISE THE SIMPLE...

—Psalm 19:7B

THE TESTIMONY OF THE LORD

God uses us to further His larger story. In the Gospel of John, it says John the Baptist came "as a witness to testify concerning that light [Jesus], so that through him all might believe." John came into this world to proclaim that the Christ has come.

See also: John 1:6–8

...THE PRECEPTS OF THE LORD ARE RIGHT, REJOICING THE HEART...

—Psalm 19:8A

THE PRECEPTS OF THE LORD

Call it what you will, but there is an impulse within the human heart that whispers something like, "go ahead, do it" when you know you shouldn't. Paul called this powerful contrarian impulse sin where "I do not do what I want, but I do the very thing I hate."

See also: Romans 7:15

...THE COMMANDMENT OF THE LORD IS PURE, ENLIGHTENING THE EYES...

—Psalm 19:8B

THE COMMANDMENT OF THE LORD

To live by the "commandment of the Lord" is to walk in the light; "God is light, and in him there is no darkness at all...if we walk in the light, as he is in the light, we have fellowship with one another, and the blood of Jesus cleanses us from all sin."

See also: 1 John 1:7

...THE FEAR OF THE LORD IS CLEAN, ENDURING FOREVER... —*Psalm 19:9A*

THE FEAR OF THE LORD

As a child, I feared the dark. This fear lingered for years. But here, the word "fear" means reverence for God and much more. "Fear of the Lord" comes upon us when we embrace the truth that God is real, powerful, and present. Without Him, we tend to become vulnerable and haunted.

See also: Psalm 52:7

...THE RULES OF THE LORD ARE TRUE, AND RIGHTEOUS ALTOGETHER.

—Psalm 19:9B

THE RULES OF THE LORD

In Jesus' time, the Jewish leaders were obsessed with total control. They used the law not to promote justice and fairness, but to protect their own power, prerogatives, and position. Their corruption bent God's law into tools for self–dealing and worse.

See also: Matthew 24:11

LET THE WORDS OF MY MOUTH AND THE MEDITATION OF MY HEART BE
ACCEPTABLE IN YOUR SIGHT, O LORD, MY ROCK AND MY REDEEMER.

—Psalm 19:14

MY PRAYER

May I, in all circumstances, abide by the words Jesus spoke to his disciples on the
night of his greatest crisis: "As the Father has loved me, so have I loved you. Abide
in my love," abide in his love; this is the love of the great commandment.

See also: John 15:9

MAY THE LORD ANSWER YOU IN THE DAY OF TROUBLE! MAY THE NAME OF THE GOD OF JACOB PROTECT YOU! —*Psalm 20:1*

PROTECT ME, LORD

The delusion of invulnerability is common in good times when we are tempted to believe in our own strength. But consider Job. He was a good man, rich and blessed when all that suddenly vanishes. Job says, "I am not at ease, nor am I quiet; I have no rest, but trouble comes."

See also: Job 3:26

MAY WE SHOUT FOR JOY OVER YOUR SALVATION, AND IN THE NAME OF OUR GOD SET UP OUR BANNERS! MAY THE LORD FULFILL ALL YOUR PETITIONS! NOW I KNOW THAT THE LORD SAVES HIS ANOINTED; HE WILL ANSWER HIM FROM HIS HOLY HEAVEN WITH THE SAVING MIGHT OF HIS RIGHT HAND. —*Psalm 20:5–6*

SHOUTS OF JOY

Once long ago, I became lost in the woods. I knew where I needed to get to, but then, I came to a fork: Which is the right path? I picked one, and bingo, I chose well. I was "saved" in a very minor way. I literally shouted for joy! Just think if it had been a life or death situation.

See also: Psalm 119:176, Luke 15:4

SOME TRUST IN CHARIOTS AND SOME IN HORSES, BUT WE TRUST IN THE NAME OF THE LORD OUR GOD. —*Psalm 20:7*

TRUST IN GOD

How difficult it is when our reason to trust disappears. People become incapacitated by fear and suspicion as danger would seem to lurk around every corner. When the people banish God, a blanket of fear settles over our lives and even the land itself.

See also: Psalm 118:5–9

MY GOD, MY GOD, WHY HAVE YOU FORSAKEN ME? WHY ARE YOU SO FAR FROM SAVING ME, FROM THE WORDS OF MY GROANING? —*Psalm 22:1*

MY GOD, MY GOD

"Eli, Eli, lama sabachthani?" (My God, my God, why have you forsaken me?) These are the words of Jesus from the cross. "The earth trembled because the Son of God humbled himself unto death, even death on a cross, so that we might live."

See also: Philippians 2:8

BE NOT FAR FROM ME, FOR TROUBLE IS NEAR, AND THERE IS NONE TO HELP. —*Psalm 22:11*

TROUBLE IS NEAR

Being nailed to a cross is a form of extreme torture invented by the Romans to humiliate the "criminal" while instilling fear in the hearts of all witnesses. Even worse than the suffering is the terrifying reality of complete abandonment. The horror of it cannot be overstated.

See also: Mark 15:16–32

ALL THE ENDS OF THE EARTH SHALL REMEMBER AND TURN TO THE LORD,

AND ALL THE FAMILIES OF THE NATIONS SHALL WORSHIP BEFORE YOU.

—Psalm 22:27

ALL PEOPLES SHALL REMEMBER

Our time on earth is bracketed by two question marks. The first is the mystery of our birth and the questions that flow from it. The second is the mystery of our death and the questions surrounding it. We sense there are answers, but are we looking in the right places?

See also: 1 Timothy 6:10

FOR KINGSHIP BELONGS TO THE LORD, AND HE RULES OVER THE NATIONS.

—Psalm 22:28

THE KING

And Jesus, the King of kings, will return: He said, "Behold, I am coming soon, bringing my recompense with me to repay each one for what he has done. I am the Alpha and the Omega, the first and the last, the beginning and the end."

See also: Revelation 22:12–13

POSTERITY SHALL SERVE HIM; IT SHALL BE TOLD OF THE LORD TO THE COMING GENERATION; THEY SHALL COME AND PROCLAIM HIS RIGHTEOUSNESS TO A PEOPLE YET UNBORN, THAT HE HAS DONE IT.

—Psalm 22:30–31

TELL THE COMING GENERATION

As Christians, we have an important task gifted to us, and it is summarized by the word "tell." The story of God's grace should never be buried. Somehow, someone passed it along to us, and we need to share it generously with others and through them with people yet unborn.

See also: Psalm 78:1–4

THE LORD IS MY SHEPHERD; I SHALL NOT WANT. HE MAKES ME LIE DOWN IN GREEN PASTURES. HE LEADS ME BESIDE STILL WATERS. HE RESTORES MY SOUL. HE LEADS ME IN PATHS OF RIGHTEOUSNESS FOR HIS NAME'S SAKE.

—Psalm 23:1–3

THE LORD IS MY SHEPHERD

The night Jesus was born, "shepherds were out in the field keeping watch over their flock by night." Jesus is the "lamb of God who takes away the sin of the world," and he is the "lamb that is led to the slaughter." He is the lamb who has been born to die so that we might live.

See also: Luke 2:8–20

THE EARTH IS THE LORD'S AND THE FULLNESS THEREOF, THE WORLD AND THOSE WHO DWELL THEREIN, FOR HE HAS FOUNDED IT UPON THE SEAS AND ESTABLISHED IT UPON THE RIVERS. —*Psalm 24:1–2*

THE EARTH IS THE LORD'S

How can we live in harmony with the Lord? The psalmist says we need to live with a pure heart and clean hands and reject what is false. But living in harmony with God also means avoiding the "cares of the world and the deceitfulness of riches and the desires for other things."

See also: Mark 4:13–20

LIFT UP YOUR HEADS, O GATES! AND BE LIFTED UP, O ANCIENT DOORS, THAT THE KING OF GLORY MAY COME IN. WHO IS THIS KING OF GLORY? THE LORD, STRONG AND MIGHTY, THE LORD, MIGHTY IN BATTLE! —*Psalm 24:7–8*

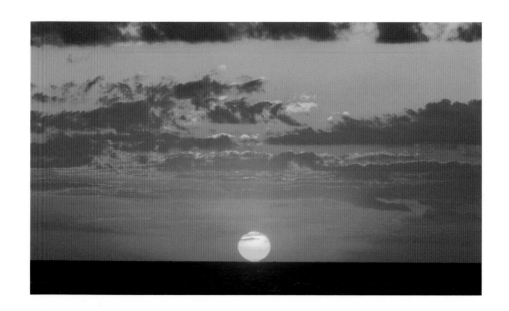

THE KING OF GLORY

Many of his followers used the word "glory" in describing Jesus; James, for example, calls him the "Lord of Glory," and the author of Hebrews says, "He is the radiance of the glory of God and the exact imprint of his nature..." This radiant glory is the light we truly need to follow.

See also: Hebrews 1:1–4

TO YOU, O LORD, I LIFT UP MY SOUL. O MY GOD, IN YOU I TRUST; LET ME NOT

BE PUT TO SHAME; LET NOT MY ENEMIES EXULT OVER ME. —*Psalm 25:1–2*

IN GOD I TRUST

What does it mean to trust God completely? It means God is your primary source of trust. You look to God first for direction, and you follow him first, even when the cacophony of voices would beckon you to follow anything but God's good way.

See also: Mark 10: 20–27

MAKE ME TO KNOW YOUR WAYS, O LORD; TEACH ME YOUR PATHS. LEAD ME IN YOUR TRUTH AND TEACH ME, FOR YOU ARE THE GOD OF MY SALVATION; FOR YOU I WAIT ALL THE DAY LONG. *—Psalm 25:4–5*

TEACH ME YOUR PATHS

Peter denies Christ in a moment of crisis. He has turned from bravado to cowardice. But after the Ascension of Jesus, Peter becomes genuinely bold before a crowd in Jerusalem and, in part, says that Jesus has made known to him the path of life. Christ Jesus is that path.

See also: Act 2:22–41

THE FRIENDSHIP OF THE LORD IS FOR THOSE WHO FEAR HIM, AND HE MAKES KNOWN TO THEM HIS COVENANT. —*Psalm 25:14*

FRIENDSHIP WITH GOD

Many today think of God as far away or even non–existent. At the same time, they will claim they are "spiritual." What's going on? By disassociating themselves from God, they are licensing themselves to be their own God, giving themselves permission to do anything they want.

See also: Galatians 5:16–24

O LORD, I LOVE THE HABITATION OF YOUR HOUSE AND THE PLACE WHERE YOUR GLORY DWELLS. —*Psalm 26:8*

GOD AMONGST US

The Temple in Jerusalem was a physical manifestation of God among us. Jesus' sacrifice radically redefines the meaning of what the temple is. Through the power of the Holy Spirit, God moves into receptive hearts, allowing the Holy Spirit to dwell within the hearts of those who believe.

See also: Corinthians 6:19–20

THE LORD IS MY LIGHT AND MY SALVATION; WHOM SHALL I FEAR? THE
LORD IS THE STRONGHOLD OF MY LIFE; OF WHOM SHALL I BE AFRAID?

—Psalm 27:1

WHOM SHALL I FEAR?

We need a Protector, especially in a world that rejects God in favor of pursuing the
darker inclinations of the heart. We should never overthrow the reality of our need
for God. Without a Savior, the world will prevail where "Malicious witnesses rise up."

See also: Psalm 35:11, 1 Timothy 6:3–5

ONE THING HAVE I ASKED OF THE LORD, THAT WILL I SEEK AFTER: THAT I MAY DWELL IN THE HOUSE OF THE LORD ALL THE DAYS OF MY LIFE, TO GAZE UPON THE BEAUTY OF THE LORD AND TO INQUIRE IN HIS TEMPLE.

—Psalm 27:4

THE BEAUTY OF THE LORD

What is beautiful to us? A glorious sunset? Snow packed mountain peaks? Yes, these are aspects of beauty. The psalmist says that God is the "perfection of beauty." Put another way God is the source of beauty. He is the Creator and we marvel at glimmers of his workmanship.

See also: Psalm 50:2, Lamentations 2:15

I BELIEVE THAT I SHALL LOOK UPON THE GOODNESS OF THE LORD IN THE LAND OF THE LIVING! WAIT FOR THE LORD; BE STRONG, AND LET YOUR HEART TAKE COURAGE; WAIT FOR THE LORD! —*Psalm 27:13–14*

WAIT FOR THE LORD

700 years. That was the span of time between Micah's prophetic words and the moment when Mary would gently place her newborn in a manger. Micah says that out of Bethlehem will come a ruler "whose origins are from of old, from ancient times." The time had finally arrived.

See also: Micah 5:2

HEAR THE VOICE OF MY PLEAS FOR MERCY, WHEN I CRY TO YOU FOR HELP,

WHEN I LIFT UP MY HANDS TOWARD YOUR MOST HOLY SANCTUARY.

—Psalm 28:2

HEAR MY PRAYER

The psalmist's "cry for help" is answered by the soft cry of a baby wrapped in cloths as protection from the cold of a winter's night. Here is a stark contrast of God's way to our way. Kings are normally born in palaces; here, a King is born in the shelter of a stable.

See also: Matthew 1:18–25, Luke2: 1–21

THE LORD IS MY STRENGTH AND MY SHIELD; IN HIM MY HEART TRUSTS, AND I AM HELPED; MY HEART EXULTS, AND WITH MY SONG I GIVE THANKS TO HIM. —*Psalm 28:7*

MY HEART EXALTS

God loves the ordinary. Nehemiah is a cupbearer to the king, but God has plans for him. Nehemiah is overwhelmed at the enormity of the task yet he knows how the impossible will get done: He says to the people "do not be grieved, for the joy of the Lord is your strength."

See also: Nehemiah 8:10

THE LORD IS THE STRENGTH OF HIS PEOPLE; HE IS THE SAVING REFUGE OF HIS ANOINTED. OH, SAVE YOUR PEOPLE AND BLESS YOUR HERITAGE! BE THEIR SHEPHERD AND CARRY THEM FOREVER. —*Psalm 28:8–9*

A SAVING REFUGE

The Lord sends his only Son into the world as an answer to the psalmist's prayer: "I am the good shepherd; I know my own and my own know me, just as the Father knows me and I know the Father; and I lay down my life for the sheep."

See also: John 10:14–15

ASCRIBE TO THE LORD, O HEAVENLY BEINGS, ASCRIBE TO THE LORD GLORY AND STRENGTH. ASCRIBE TO THE LORD THE GLORY DUE HIS NAME; WORSHIP THE LORD IN THE SPLENDOR OF HOLINESS. —*Psalm 29:1–2*

THE SPLENDOR OF GOD'S HOLINESS

The world may counsel us differently, but Peter provides a powerful reason to strive for the "splendor of holiness" in all we do. Quoting Leviticus, he says that we should pursue holiness, for the Lord your God is holy. And God provides the perfect model of holiness: Jesus Christ.

See also: Leviticus 20:7, 1 Peter 1:16

THE LORD SITS ENTHRONED OVER THE FLOOD; THE LORD SITS ENTHRONED AS KING FOREVER. MAY THE LORD GIVE STRENGTH TO HIS PEOPLE! MAY THE LORD BLESS HIS PEOPLE WITH PEACE! —*Psalm 29:10–11*

THE LORD IS KING FOREVER

How easy it is to forget who the actual King is. The psalmist remembers however. The Lord is enthroned over the earth; He is King forever, and we will be blessed when we finally acknowledge where our true strength comes from.

See also: Psalm 28:7

O LORD MY GOD, I CRIED TO YOU FOR HELP, AND YOU HAVE HEALED ME. O LORD, YOU HAVE BROUGHT UP MY SOUL FROM SHEOL; YOU RESTORED ME TO LIFE FROM AMONG THOSE WHO GO DOWN TO THE PIT. —*Psalm 30:2–3*

YOU HAVE HEALED ME, O GOD

These words touch me with the deepest gratitude. I have said the Lord blessed me through my despair over failure. The normal words of solace could not reach me. It was the Lord who lifted me out of the muck and mire; He surely had plans for me that I knew nothing about at that moment.

See also: Jeremiah 29:11–14

SING PRAISES TO THE LORD, O YOU HIS SAINTS, AND GIVE THANKS TO HIS HOLY NAME. FOR HIS ANGER IS BUT FOR A MOMENT, AND HIS FAVOR IS FOR A LIFETIME. WEEPING MAY TARRY FOR THE NIGHT, BUT JOY COMES WITH THE MORNING. —*Psalm 30:4–5*

JOY COMES WITH THE MORNING

Joy comes with the morning when we realize that the Lord has been near as we slept, watching over us, and even speaking to us through our dreams. His "steadfast love never ceases; his mercies never come to an end; they are new every morning."

See also: Lamentations 3:22–23

HEAR, O LORD, AND BE MERCIFUL TO ME! O LORD, BE MY HELPER! YOU HAVE TURNED FOR ME MY MOURNING INTO DANCING; YOU HAVE LOOSED MY SACKCLOTH AND CLOTHED ME WITH GLADNESS, —*Psalm 30:10–11*

O LORD, BE MY HELPER

The poetry of the Psalms reinforces a sense of our longing for that which is good. But while we see glimpses of the beauty and harmony in nature and the universe, we often default to the jarring discords around us, and we become clothed in unhappiness and not gladness.

See also: Psalm 27:4

IN YOU, O LORD, DO I TAKE REFUGE; LET ME NEVER BE PUT TO SHAME; IN YOUR RIGHTEOUSNESS DELIVER ME! INCLINE YOUR EAR TO ME; RESCUE ME SPEEDILY! BE A ROCK OF REFUGE FOR ME, A STRONG FORTRESS TO SAVE ME!

—Psalm 31:1–2

THE LORD IS MY REFUGE

Storms occur on many levels. I am writing this because at one time I found myself in a spiritual battle of biblical proportions, at least for me. I found myself exposed and vulnerable in the extreme. All seemed lost, but it did not turn out that way. The Lord was near.

See also: Psalm 18:4–19

INTO YOUR HAND I COMMIT MY SPIRIT; YOU HAVE REDEEMED ME, O LORD, FAITHFUL GOD. —*Psalm 31:5*

LORD, I COMMIT MY SPIRIT TO YOU

Jesus said these very words from the cross: "'Father into your hands I commit my spirit.' And having said this he breathed his last." In the agony of death, Jesus does not turn on his Father. He knows his mission is to die for many, and his mission is now complete.

See also: Luke 23:46

BE GRACIOUS TO ME, O LORD, FOR I AM IN DISTRESS; MY EYE IS WASTED FROM GRIEF; MY SOUL AND MY BODY ALSO. —*Psalm 31:9*

GOD'S GRACE

God's grace flows like a mighty torrent when we invite him into our hearts. But many fear their local identity will be swept away. And so, tragically, this fear of losing something impermanent inhibits the desire to accept the eternal gift God has offered each of us.

See also: Ephesians 2:4–10

OH, HOW ABUNDANT IS YOUR GOODNESS, WHICH YOU HAVE STORED UP FOR THOSE WHO FEAR YOU AND WORKED FOR THOSE WHO TAKE REFUGE IN YOU, IN THE SIGHT OF THE CHILDREN OF MANKIND! —*Psalm 31:19*

YOUR ABUNDANT GOODNESS

The chasm separating the goodness of material abundance and the abundance of the "goodness flowing from God" is bottomless. The abundance that flows from God has eternal roots, but the abundance of wealth is as fleeting a cloud's shadow passing across a windswept plain.

See also: Galatians 5:22–26

BE STRONG, AND LET YOUR HEART TAKE COURAGE, ALL YOU WHO WAIT FOR THE LORD! —*Psalm 31:24*

BE STRONG

To be strong in the Lord looks like this: "...to fear the Lord your God, to walk in all his ways, to love him, to serve the Lord your God with all your heart and with all your soul, and to keep the commandments and statutes of the Lord...."

See also: Deuteronomy 10:12–13

BLESSED IS THE ONE WHOSE TRANSGRESSION IS FORGIVEN, WHOSE SIN IS COVERED. BLESSED IS THE MAN AGAINST WHOM THE LORD COUNTS NO INIQUITY, AND IN WHOSE SPIRIT THERE IS NO DECEIT. —*Psalm 32:1–2*

GOD WILL FORGIVE

Think of forgiveness on two levels: Peace with God leading to peace in your own heart. If you are not at peace with God, you cannot have peace because your heart will remain broken and frayed. Many of the "forgiveness substitutes" offered today are very weak remedies indeed.

See also: Jeremiah 17:9

I ACKNOWLEDGED MY SIN TO YOU, AND I DID NOT COVER MY INIQUITY; I SAID, "I WILL CONFESS MY TRANSGRESSIONS TO THE LORD," AND YOU FORGAVE THE INIQUITY OF MY SIN. —*Psalm 32:5*

I CONFESSED

Another word that has lost favor in our own times is "confession." We say "I'm sorry" all the time as a weak substitute, but wouldn't it be better to remember the words of David in his confessional psalm? Ask God first for forgiveness, then seek out those you have wronged.

See also: Psalm 51:4

YOU ARE A HIDING PLACE FOR ME; YOU PRESERVE ME FROM TROUBLE; YOU SURROUND ME WITH SHOUTS OF DELIVERANCE. —*Psalm 32:7*

YOU ARE MY HIDING PLACE

Corrie ten Boom lived a quiet life in a quiet corner of the Netherlands. Then, the spell of safety was shattered with the Nazi invasion in 1940. Corrie wrote a book called *The Hiding Place* where she shows what it means to have God near when you are imperiled by overpowering evil.

See also: Lamentations 3:1–23

MANY ARE THE SORROWS OF THE WICKED, BUT STEADFAST LOVE SURROUNDS THE ONE WHO TRUSTS IN THE LORD. BE GLAD IN THE LORD, AND REJOICE, O RIGHTEOUS, AND SHOUT FOR JOY, ALL YOU UPRIGHT IN HEART! —*Psalm 32:10–11*

SHOUT FOR JOY

The psalmist says, "Be glad in the Lord." Paul says to us, "be filled with the Spirit, addressing one another in psalms and hymns and spiritual songs...giving thanks always and for everything to God the Father in the name of our Lord Jesus Christ..."

See also: Ephesians 5:19–20

FOR THE WORD OF THE LORD IS UPRIGHT, AND ALL HIS WORK IS DONE IN FAITHFULNESS. HE LOVES RIGHTEOUSNESS AND JUSTICE; THE EARTH IS FULL OF THE STEADFAST LOVE OF THE LORD. —*Psalm 33:4–5*

THE WORD WAS GOD

Jesus and the Word of God are one and the same. John declares this truth in the opening of his gospel: "In the beginning was the Word, and the Word was with God, and the Word was God." And Jesus says: "Father, glorify me...with the glory I had with you before the world began."

See also: John 1:1, John 17:5

BEHOLD, THE EYE OF THE LORD IS ON THOSE WHO FEAR HIM, ON THOSE WHO HOPE IN HIS STEADFAST LOVE, THAT HE MAY DELIVER THEIR SOUL FROM DEATH AND KEEP THEM ALIVE IN FAMINE. —*Psalm 33:18–19*

THE EYE OF THE LORD

Jesus sends a message to the imprisoned John the Baptist that he should not despair: "Go and tell John what you hear and see," and then adds, "blessed is the one who is not offended by me." Many remain "offended" by Jesus, but those who do believe can "see" the truth and spread it.

See also: John 7:25–31

I WILL BLESS THE LORD AT ALL TIMES; HIS PRAISE SHALL CONTINUALLY BE IN MY MOUTH. MY SOUL MAKES ITS BOAST IN THE LORD; LET THE HUMBLE HEAR AND BE GLAD. —*Psalm 34:1–2*

HEAR AND BE GLAD

"I will bless the Lord at all times" means I will bless him in season and out. I will bless him on rainy days when I prayed for sunny days. I will bless him with my life by following him whether the way be rough or smooth. And I will bless him for what his Son did for me and for you.

See also: Psalm 103:1–13

THE ANGEL OF THE LORD ENCAMPS AROUND THOSE WHO FEAR HIM, AND DELIVERS THEM. OH, TASTE AND SEE THAT THE LORD IS GOOD! BLESSED IS THE MAN WHO TAKES REFUGE IN HIM! —*Psalm 34:7–8*

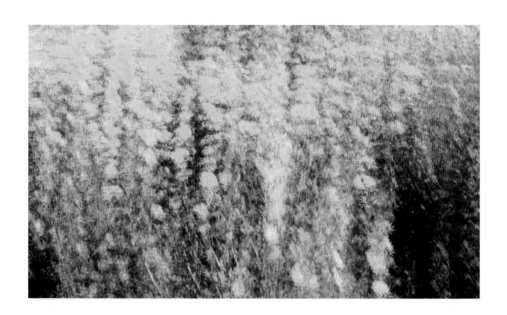

OH, TASTE AND SEE

This reference to "the angel of the Lord" reminds me of Elisha's prayer: "'O Lord, please open his eyes that he might see.' So the Lord opened the eyes of the young man, and he saw, and behold, the mountain was full of horses and chariots of fire all around Elisha."

See also: 2 Kings 6:17

THE LORD IS NEAR TO THE BROKENHEARTED AND SAVES THE CRUSHED IN SPIRIT. MANY ARE THE AFFLICTIONS OF THE RIGHTEOUS, BUT THE LORD DELIVERS HIM OUT OF THEM ALL. *—Psalm 34:18–19*

THE LORD IS NEAR

Trouble came in waves; I clung to the wreckage of my career until I submerged into hopelessness. In desperation, I cried out to God and I "miraculously" survived. This may sound counterintuitive, but I now bless those terrible days because out of the bad, much good has followed.

See also: John 16:32

THE LORD REDEEMS THE LIFE OF HIS SERVANTS; NONE OF THOSE WHO TAKE REFUGE IN HIM WILL BE CONDEMNED. —*Psalm 34:22*

MERCY

Jesus was born to die, not for himself as a martyr, but as the Son of God who died as a willing sacrifice for you and for me for "[Mary] will bear a son and you shall call his name Jesus, for he will save his people from their sins."

See also: Matthew 1:18–25

HOW LONG, O LORD, WILL YOU LOOK ON? RESCUE ME FROM THEIR DESTRUCTION, MY PRECIOUS LIFE FROM THE LIONS! I WILL THANK YOU IN THE GREAT CONGREGATION; IN THE MIGHTY THRONG I WILL PRAISE YOU.

—Psalm 35:17–18

RESCUE ME, LORD

Sometimes desperation brings the language of the spirit of God to life in our hearts. The dormant seed is within us, but that seed will not sprout unless we overcome our resistance and say, "Come, Holy Spirit, come." And then, God's Word, the Bible, can become THE book, not a book.

See also: Revelation 22:16–21

LET NOT THOSE REJOICE OVER ME WHO ARE WRONGFULLY MY FOES, AND
LET NOT THOSE WINK THE EYE WHO HATE ME WITHOUT CAUSE.

—Psalm 35:19

HATRED WITHOUT CAUSE

In our time, we use "science" to explain everything. And we are uncomfortable
when we cannot rationalize our actions. But still, the deep motives of the heart
remain beyond reach: "The heart is deceitful above all things, and desperately sick;
who can understand it?"

See also: Jeremiah 17:9

LET THOSE WHO DELIGHT IN MY RIGHTEOUSNESS SHOUT FOR JOY AND BE GLAD AND SAY EVERMORE, "GREAT IS THE LORD, WHO DELIGHTS IN THE WELFARE OF HIS SERVANT!" —*Psalm 35:27*

GREAT IS THE LORD

How incredible: God delights in us! But not because we have done great things for ourselves. He delights because we have turned away from alternative loves to loving him and believing that he loves us which is our "righteousness." Our abiding in God's love truly delights him.

See also: Genesis 1:26–31

YOUR STEADFAST LOVE, O LORD, EXTENDS TO THE HEAVENS, YOUR
FAITHFULNESS TO THE CLOUDS. —*Psalm 36:5*

GOD'S FAITHFULNESS

You would think the disciples of Jesus would be steadfast, but in Gethsemane, one
disciple betrays him, some fall asleep, and in the end, all flee. Later, Peter even denies
Jesus. So brave words are not enough. A time will come when our faithfulness will
be tested. Bank on it.

See also: Matthew 26:56

YOUR RIGHTEOUSNESS IS LIKE THE MOUNTAINS OF GOD; YOUR JUDGMENTS
ARE LIKE THE GREAT DEEP; MAN AND BEAST YOU SAVE, O LORD.

—Psalm 36:6

THE MOUNTAINS OF GOD

Mt. Moriah is where God provided Abraham a substituted sacrifice for his son. Mt.
Sinai is where God gave Moses the Ten Commandments we live by. Mt. Horeb
is where Elijah encountered God, and the hill called Golgotha is where God gave
everything so that you and I might be saved.

See also: Isaiah 2:2–3

HOW PRECIOUS IS YOUR STEADFAST LOVE, O GOD! THE CHILDREN OF MANKIND TAKE REFUGE IN THE SHADOW OF YOUR WINGS. FOR WITH YOU IS THE FOUNTAIN OF LIFE; IN YOUR LIGHT DO WE SEE LIGHT. —*Psalm 36:7,9*

THE LIGHT OF GOD'S LOVE

Without light there is no life. At creation, God said, "Let there be light..." But Adam's choice opened the human heart to a darkness that would attack the light. So, God sent light in the person of Jesus to set in motion the restoration of the light of Christ in the human heart.

See also: 2 Corinthians 4:1–6

OH, CONTINUE YOUR STEADFAST LOVE TO THOSE WHO KNOW YOU, AND YOUR RIGHTEOUSNESS TO THE UPRIGHT OF HEART! —*Psalm 36:10*

GOD'S STEADFAST LOVE

When hiring a new employee, wouldn't it be good to know they are steady, solid, reliable, devoted, committed, and true. That person would be a wonderful choice. Here is the best news ever: God is all these things and more. And we can share in it if we will only ask.

See also: Luke 11:9–13

TRUST IN THE LORD, AND DO GOOD; DWELL IN THE LAND AND BEFRIEND FAITHFULNESS. DELIGHT YOURSELF IN THE LORD, AND HE WILL GIVE YOU THE DESIRES OF YOUR HEART. COMMIT YOUR WAY TO THE LORD; TRUST IN HIM, AND HE WILL ACT. —*Psalm 37:3–5*

TRUST IN THE LORD

Here is a promise worth everything: If you will trust in the Lord, dwell with him, befriend him, and delight in him, he will give you the "desires of your heart." That does not mean you will get wealth or fame. It means he will give you wisdom, joy, love, and life eternal with him.

See also: Psalm 40:1–4

THE LORD KNOWS THE DAYS OF THE BLAMELESS, AND THEIR HERITAGE WILL REMAIN FOREVER; —*Psalm 37:18*

THE DAYS OF THE BLAMELESS

The "days of the blameless" became possible only because God's one and only son, Jesus, died on a cross outside the walls of Jerusalem. He, the truly blameless one, would die as a sufficient sacrifice for each one of us so that we could become blameless in the eyes of God.

See also: 2 Corinthians 5:17–21

FOR MY INIQUITIES HAVE GONE OVER MY HEAD; LIKE A HEAVY BURDEN, THEY ARE TOO HEAVY FOR ME. —*Psalm 38:4*

A HEAVY BURDEN

As a hiker, I know how it feels to lug heavy loads over miles of rugged terrain. Unresolved sin is just like carrying a load of dead rocks long distances. You struggle, hoping to find relief, but find none. You grind out the miles thinking there must be a better way. There is.

See also: Psalm 32:1–5

O LORD, ALL MY LONGING IS BEFORE YOU; MY SIGHING IS NOT HIDDEN FROM YOU. MY HEART THROBS; MY STRENGTH FAILS ME, AND THE LIGHT OF MY EYES—IT ALSO HAS GONE FROM ME. —*Psalm 38:9–10*

MY STRENGTH FAILS ME

After killing his brother, Cain cries out, "I am a fugitive and a wanderer on the earth." His guilt pursues him. He is a hunted and a haunted man because he knows that God knows what he has done. And it is this condition of being exiled from God that is so unbearable to him.

I CONFESS MY INIQUITY; I AM SORRY FOR MY SIN. —*Psalm 38:18*

I C O N F E S S   M Y   I N I Q U I T Y

When we lie to ourselves and rationalize our poor judgment or bad behavior, we remain incapable of coming clean with God. But "If we confess our sins, God is faithful and just to forgive us our sins and to cleanse us from all unrighteousness."

See also: 1 John 1:8–9

DO NOT FORSAKE ME, O LORD! O MY GOD, BE NOT FAR FROM ME! MAKE HASTE TO HELP ME, O LORD, MY SALVATION! —*Psalm 38:21–22*

LORD, BE NOT FAR FROM ME

The consequences of the psalmist's sin have been eating away at him physically. He says he had forsaken God, but now pleads to God not to forsake him. He has taken the step toward health by confessing his sin. He knows that his salvation is from God and from God only.

See also: Psalm 51:1–11

"O LORD, MAKE ME KNOW MY END AND WHAT IS THE MEASURE OF MY DAYS; LET ME KNOW HOW FLEETING I AM! BEHOLD, YOU HAVE MADE MY DAYS A FEW HANDBREADTHS, AND MY LIFETIME IS AS NOTHING BEFORE YOU. SURELY ALL MANKIND STANDS AS A MERE BREATH!" —*Psalm 39:4–5*

THE MEASURE OF MY DAYS

Jesus tells of a man who had become rich to the point where he says, "relax, eat, drink, be merry." It is at this moment of great self–satisfaction that God says, "Fool! This night your soul is required of you." The rich man had foolishly concluded wealth is security. It is not.

See also: Luke 12:13–21

"HEAR MY PRAYER, O LORD, AND GIVE EAR TO MY CRY; HOLD NOT YOUR PEACE AT MY TEARS! FOR I AM A SOJOURNER WITH YOU, A GUEST, LIKE ALL MY FATHERS." —*Psalm 39:12*

HEAR MY PRAYER, O LORD

The psalmist declares a universal truth: Our time on earth is transitory. He says we are guests and that soon enough we will move on. But he also says that he is a "sojourner with the Lord." He has a friend who will be at his side whether the path is easy or difficult.

See also: Acts 7:6, Ephesian 5–8, 2 Timothy 2:22

I WAITED PATIENTLY FOR THE LORD; HE INCLINED TO ME AND HEARD MY CRY. HE DREW ME UP FROM THE PIT OF DESTRUCTION, OUT OF THE MIRY BOG, AND SET MY FEET UPON A ROCK, MAKING MY STEPS SECURE.

—Psalm 40:1–2

LORD, YOU SET MY FEET ON A ROCK

The promise is eternal salvation, not perfect comfort in our everyday existence. Our feet are stuck in a "miry bog," but our heart yearns for eternity. What makes our "steps secure" and our foundation a "rock" is our faith that the Lord is trustworthy. Be patient, always.

See also: James 5:7

BLESSED IS THE MAN WHO MAKES THE LORD HIS TRUST, WHO DOES NOT TURN TO THE PROUD, TO THOSE WHO GO ASTRAY AFTER A LIE! —*Psalm 40:4*

TRUST IN THE LORD

If we put our trust in a person, what are the chances of disappointment or betrayal? The biblical truth is that all people sin and fall short of the glory of God. Even Jesus' disciples abandon him even though they love him. Trusting in the Lord first puts the world right side up.

See also: Romans 3:21–25

THEN I SAID, "BEHOLD, I HAVE COME; IN THE SCROLL OF THE BOOK IT IS WRITTEN OF ME: I DELIGHT TO DO YOUR WILL, O MY GOD; YOUR LAW IS WITHIN MY HEART." —*Psalm 40:7–8*

HERE I AM, LORD

The Lord called Abraham and he answered, "Here I am." The Lord called Samuel and he answered, "Here I am!" The Lord called Isaiah and he answered, "Here I am!" The Lord called you and he called me and we answered...

See also: Genesis 22:1, 1 Samuel 3:4, Isaiah 6:8

BUT MAY ALL WHO SEEK YOU REJOICE AND BE GLAD IN YOU; MAY THOSE WHO LOVE YOUR SALVATION SAY CONTINUALLY, "GREAT IS THE LORD!"

—*Psalm 40:16*

"GREAT IS THE LORD"

We may think people naturally seek the Lord. Many do, but remember the example of Adam and Eve. After they eat the forbidden fruit, they become self–aware and afraid. They hide from God; they lie to him and blame him. Their impulsive act has put them at enmity with God.

See also: Genesis 3:6–13

AS A DEER PANTS FOR FLOWING STREAMS, SO PANTS MY SOUL FOR YOU, O GOD. MY SOUL THIRSTS FOR GOD, FOR THE LIVING GOD. WHEN SHALL I COME AND APPEAR BEFORE GOD? —*Psalm 42:1–2*

MY SOUL THIRSTS FOR GOD

While hiking, I discovered what thirst is. Quenching that thirst becomes a painful obsession. Just as with physical thirst, our soul thirst becomes real when our spiritual resources dry up. As water sustains the body, so the love of God brings life to the soul.

See also: Psalm 63:1

AS WITH A DEADLY WOUND IN MY BONES, MY ADVERSARIES TAUNT ME,
WHILE THEY SAY TO ME ALL THE DAY LONG, "WHERE IS YOUR GOD?"

—Psalm 42:10

"WHERE IS YOUR GOD?"

This verse foreshadows the plight of "the lamb of God" being taunted beyond the walls of Jerusalem. He has been brutally nailed to a cross as "the people stood by, watching, [and] the rulers scoffed at him." But they taunted not knowing that they and their master had been vanquished.

See also: Matthew 27:32–44

WHY ARE YOU CAST DOWN, O MY SOUL, AND WHY ARE YOU IN TURMOIL WITHIN ME? HOPE IN GOD; FOR I SHALL AGAIN PRAISE HIM, MY SALVATION AND MY GOD. —*Psalm 42:11*

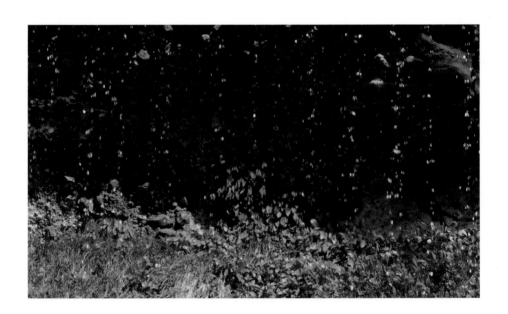

HOPE IN GOD

Depression extinguishes hope. But the psalmist says "Hope in God." Jesus confirms this because he has an eternal perspective: "Those who are well have no need for a physician, but those who are sick. I came not to call the righteous, but sinners." Jesus links physical disease and sin. We should listen to him.

See also: Mark 2:17, Matthew 9:1–8

VINDICATE ME, O GOD, AND DEFEND MY CAUSE AGAINST AN UNGODLY PEOPLE, FROM THE DECEITFUL AND UNJUST MAN DELIVER ME! —*Psalm 43:1*

AN UNGODLY PEOPLE

"Ungodliness" is a word that has disappeared from common usage. Why? Perhaps it is the distaste for discerning the good from the bad, and right from wrong. But if words become a mélange of confusions, then we are living in a Babel–like world where meaning is mangled and murdered.

SEND OUT YOUR LIGHT AND YOUR TRUTH; LET THEM LEAD ME; LET THEM BRING ME TO YOUR HOLY HILL AND TO YOUR DWELLING! —*Psalm 43:3*

LEAD ME, LORD

We need the light of the truth of God to find our way as we move toward God's holy hill. God gave Moses the Ten Commandments for the people as a light to light the way to the promised land and beyond, but they rejected God's way and so they wandered in the dry desert 40 years.

See also: Exodus 32:1–35

RISE UP; COME TO OUR HELP! REDEEM US FOR THE SAKE OF YOUR STEADFAST LOVE! —*Psalm 44:26*

REDEEM US, LORD

The psalmist says that God has turned away from his people. Earlier, he says the Lord has "rejected and disgraced us" when in earlier days he had protected them. He knows all is lost without God's steadfast hand. When he pleads "Redeem us" he is asking for the restoration of God's favor.

See also: 1 Peter 5:6–11

YOUR THRONE, O GOD, IS FOREVER AND EVER. THE SCEPTER OF YOUR KINGDOM IS A SCEPTER OF UPRIGHTNESS; —*Psalm 45:6*

YOUR KINGDOM IS FOREVER

The righteous earthly king is a reflection of the heavenly king. He is a model of what the true restored kingdom will be: "In your majesty ride out victoriously for the cause of truth and meekness and righteousness..." This is a picture of the kingdom to come.

See also: Luke 13:18–21, Luke 13:22–30

GOD IS OUR REFUGE AND STRENGTH, A VERY PRESENT HELP IN TROUBLE.

—Psalm 46:1

GOD, OUR HELP IN TROUBLE

I have many favorite psalms, and this one is near the top of the list. God is our refuge and strength even when the earth gives way, when the mountains collapse into the sea, and when the oceans roar and foam. There can be much to fear, but the Lord's favor is our strength.

See also: Psalm 28:7, Nehemiah 8:10, Psalm 118:14

THERE IS A RIVER WHOSE STREAMS MAKE GLAD THE CITY OF GOD, THE HOLY HABITATION OF THE MOST HIGH. —*Psalm 46:4*

THE CITY OF GOD

The City of God can seem far off because we actually inhabit a city constructed by the hands of mortals. We marvel at its beauty and complexity, but still, it can wear out and become an empty ruin. It's the City of God, not the city of man, that should be our desired destination.

See also: Genesis 11:1–9

SING PRAISES TO GOD, SING PRAISES! SING PRAISES TO OUR KING, SING PRAISES! FOR GOD IS THE KING OF ALL THE EARTH; SING PRAISES WITH A PSALM! —*Psalm 47:6–7*

SING PRAISES TO GOD

Who rules the world? Scientists acknowledge physical laws exist to regulate the sun, the moon, the planets, and the stars, but there are spiritual laws that are just as real and important. And these laws deserve our praise and adulation for the King of kings, who created it all.

See also: Mark 16:15

GREAT IS THE LORD AND GREATLY TO BE PRAISED IN THE CITY OF OUR GOD! HIS HOLY MOUNTAIN, BEAUTIFUL IN ELEVATION, IS THE JOY OF ALL THE EARTH, MOUNT ZION, IN THE FAR NORTH, THE CITY OF THE GREAT KING. *—Psalm 48:1–2*

GREAT IS THE LORD

How are we to behold David's City? Has any other city been so central to the often conflicted relationship between God and his people, a people who both served God and rebelled against him? Has any place on earth been so central to the essential story of our human destiny?

See also: Luke 13:34

WALK ABOUT ZION, GO AROUND HER, NUMBER HER TOWERS, CONSIDER WELL HER RAMPARTS, GO THROUGH HER CITADELS, THAT YOU MAY TELL THE NEXT GENERATION THAT THIS IS GOD, OUR GOD FOREVER AND EVER. HE WILL GUIDE US FOREVER. —*Psalm 48:12–14*

TELL THE NEXT GENERATION

What are we telling our next generation? Will they build on our wealth or squander it? Will they inherit a sense of purpose and direction or will they be content to descend into self–indulgent hedonism? Will they seek God or deny him? What we do today will touch tomorrow.

See also: Matthew 28:16–20, Acts 23:11

MAN IN HIS POMP YET WITHOUT UNDERSTANDING IS LIKE THE BEASTS THAT PERISH. —*Psalm 49:20*

PRIDE

Man in his pomp is a creature suffused with pride. Pride is deadly as it serves as a barrier to the reality beyond mere self. Pride blinds us, and so, we wander from here to there aimlessly doing this and that with no clear purpose to our wanderings beyond self–aggrandizement.

See also: Luke 6:39

THE MIGHTY ONE, GOD THE LORD, SPEAKS AND SUMMONS THE EARTH FROM THE RISING OF THE SUN TO ITS SETTING. —*Psalm 50:1*

GOD IS LORD

Visually, sunrise and sunset are the most dramatic moments of the day. It is as if the glory of God reveals itself in an array of dramatic reds and oranges to announce the beauty of the creation all over again. God said, "Let there be light," and we are reminded of that daily.

See also: John 8:12–20

AND CALL UPON ME IN THE DAY OF TROUBLE; I WILL DELIVER YOU, AND YOU SHALL GLORIFY ME. —*Psalm 50:15*

I WILL DELIVER YOU

I was a child of my times. The Bible was a book on a shelf: unopened, unread, unknown. Then, life intruded and I was awakened to the need to act or be destroyed. I instinctively turned to God in prayer. God did act, changing everything, including my heart, my mind, and my purpose.

See also: Psalm 34:7

HAVE MERCY ON ME, O GOD, ACCORDING TO YOUR STEADFAST LOVE;
ACCORDING TO YOUR ABUNDANT MERCY BLOT OUT MY TRANSGRESSIONS.

—Psalm 51:1

A PLEA FOR MERCY

King David, at the height of his kingly power, commits a series of crimes and then tries to cover them up. He has betrayed God on multiple levels, and he tries to hide the truth even from himself. Here, David is confessing his grievous sins and is pleading to God for mercy.

See also: 2 Samuel 12:1–12

CREATE IN ME A CLEAN HEART, O GOD, AND RENEW A RIGHT SPIRIT WITHIN ME. CAST ME NOT AWAY FROM YOUR PRESENCE, AND TAKE NOT YOUR HOLY SPIRIT FROM ME. —*Psalm 51:10–11*

A SINNER'S PLEA

David has sinned. He acted on his desire for another man's wife and compounded that crime by having Uriah, her husband, killed. David has given up rationalizing his crime. His sins have exiled him from God's grace. He begs God to restore access to His Holy Spirit.

See also: 2 Samuel 12:13–15

BUT I AM LIKE A GREEN OLIVE TREE IN THE HOUSE OF GOD. I TRUST IN THE STEADFAST LOVE OF GOD FOREVER AND EVER. —*Psalm 52:8*

I TRUST IN GOD

If we choose not to trust in God, we will most certainly find substitutes of one kind or another to trust, the most obvious being money. The parable of the rich fool ends in disaster when God proclaims, "You fool! This very night your life will be demanded of you."

See also: Luke 12:13–21

THE FOOL SAYS IN HIS HEART, "THERE IS NO GOD." THEY ARE CORRUPT,

DOING ABOMINABLE INIQUITY; THERE IS NONE WHO DOES GOOD.

—Psalm 53:1

A FOOLISH HEART

As faith in science grew in the 19th century, the "wise men" of those times turned the psalmist's declaration upside down: The fool to them is he who says God exists. But what is the track record? On one side, "God is love" while on the other are stockpiles of weapons of mass destruction.

See also: 1 Corinthians 1:18–25, 1 John 4:7–21

OH, THAT SALVATION FOR ISRAEL WOULD COME OUT OF ZION! WHEN GOD RESTORES THE FORTUNES OF HIS PEOPLE, LET JACOB REJOICE, LET ISRAEL BE GLAD. —*Psalm 53:6*

LET ISRAEL BE GLAD

Christians believe that a life well lived is about redemption, not "progress." This is not a popular idea today, but with Christ, human history turned toward restoration through the cross. When we say we can build a better world on our own strength, we are badly deceived.

See also: Psalm 2:1–3, John 3:35–36

GIVE EAR TO MY PRAYER, O GOD, AND HIDE NOT YOURSELF FROM MY PLEA FOR MERCY! —*Psalm 55:1*

MY PLEA FOR MERCY

Jesus prayed continuously to the Father. From the beginning, Jesus is on his father's mission to redeem all from the grip of sin. As his time approaches, he prays, "Father, glorify me in your presence with the glory I had with you before the world began."

See also: John 17:5

FOR IT IS NOT AN ENEMY WHO TAUNTS ME—THEN I COULD BEAR IT; IT IS NOT AN ADVERSARY WHO DEALS INSOLENTLY WITH ME—THEN I COULD HIDE FROM HIM. BUT IT IS YOU, A MAN, MY EQUAL, MY COMPANION, MY FAMILIAR FRIEND. —*Psalm 55:12–13*

MY FAMILIAR FRIEND

A sin–sick world is marked by betrayal. Adam and Eve betray God; Cain betrays his brother; Absalom betrays his father David, and Jesus is betrayed by every one of his disciples. Betrayal is faithlessness, even while God is relentlessly faithful.

See also: Matthew 26:47–56

CAST YOUR BURDEN ON THE LORD, AND HE WILL SUSTAIN YOU; HE WILL NEVER PERMIT THE RIGHTEOUS TO BE MOVED. —*Psalm 55:22*

GOD WILL SUSTAIN YOU

Jesus offers to "cast our cares" upon him. He will be our help: "Come to me, all you who are weary and burdened, and I will give you rest. Take my yoke upon you and learn from me, for I am gentle and humble in heart, and you will find rest for your souls."

See also: Matthew 11:28–29

WHEN I AM AFRAID, I PUT MY TRUST IN YOU. IN GOD, WHOSE WORD I PRAISE,

IN GOD I TRUST; I SHALL NOT BE AFRAID. WHAT CAN FLESH DO TO ME?

—Psalm 56:3–4

IN GOD I TRUST

Banks are often called "Trust Companies". We need assurance that the managers will be honest. As Christians, we are called to trust Jesus just as he trusted God completely. How can we follow Jesus if we do not totally trust him? Lord, help me to overcome my inclination to distrust.

See also: Mark 9:24

IN GOD, WHOSE WORD I PRAISE, IN THE LORD, WHOSE WORD I PRAISE, IN
GOD I TRUST; I SHALL NOT BE AFRAID. WHAT CAN MAN DO TO ME?

—Psalm 56:10–11

BE NOT AFRAID

Fear is the great murderer of faith. Even in Gethsemane, as he is praying to the
Father, Jesus does not express fear. He says, "My soul is sorrowful, even to death,"
but then to the Father, he says, "not as I will, but as you will." Jesus knows he must
trust his Father completely.

See also: Isaiah 44:6–8

"FOR YOU HAVE DELIVERED MY SOUL FROM DEATH, YES, MY FEET FROM FALLING, THAT I MAY WALK BEFORE GOD IN THE LIGHT OF LIFE."

—*Psalm 56:13*

THE LIGHT OF LIFE

The further we wander from God, the greater the danger that we will become hopelessly lost. The psalmist says "Your word is a lamp for my feet and a light for my path." Jesus is that light that overcomes the power of the darkness that enshrouds and afflicts the whole world.

See also: Psalm 119:105–111

BE MERCIFUL TO ME, O GOD, BE MERCIFUL TO ME, FOR IN YOU MY SOUL TAKES REFUGE; IN THE SHADOW OF YOUR WINGS I WILL TAKE REFUGE, TILL THE STORMS OF DESTRUCTION PASS BY. —*Psalm 57:1*

BE MERCIFUL TO ME, O GOD

Anyone who asks for God's mercy has traveled a long road from self–sufficiency to a realization that without God there can be no hope and no exit. It is often when our previous assumptions lie in tatters that we find that God is real and the life we once lived is not.

See also: John 9:24–34

I WILL GIVE THANKS TO YOU, O LORD, AMONG THE PEOPLES; I WILL SING PRAISES TO YOU AMONG THE NATIONS. FOR YOUR STEADFAST LOVE IS GREAT TO THE HEAVENS, YOUR FAITHFULNESS TO THE CLOUDS.

—Psalm 57:9–11

GIVE THANKS TO THE LORD

The psalmist cannot contain his joy. He sings praises to God's steadfast love and faithfulness for the peoples. Compare that to our own lukewarm gratitude for God's boundless grace. God's love and faithfulness hasn't changed, but our buttoned down response seems very tame indeed.

See also: Revelation 3:15–16

BUT I WILL SING OF YOUR STRENGTH; I WILL SING ALOUD OF YOUR STEADFAST LOVE IN THE MORNING. FOR YOU HAVE BEEN TO ME A FORTRESS AND A REFUGE IN THE DAY OF MY DISTRESS. —*Psalm 59:16*

YOU ARE MY REFUGE, O GOD

Jesus is our refuge. We call upon him when the world seems to be crashing down upon us, but what about Jesus himself? Jesus did not depend upon himself, but looked to God always: "For I have not spoken on my own authority...What I say, therefore, I say as the Father has told me."

See also: John 12:44–50

OH, GRANT US HELP AGAINST THE FOE, FOR VAIN IS THE SALVATION OF MAN! —*Psalm 60:11*

GRANT US HELP, O LORD

How do we think about "the salvation of man"? What is our horizon? Are we thinking about today only or tomorrow? Do we think about next week or next month or next year? Or are we so stuck in the now that we avoid time and eternity altogether? It is possible to get lost in the present.

See also: 2 Peter 3:18

WITH GOD WE SHALL DO VALIANTLY; IT IS HE WHO WILL TREAD DOWN OUR FOES. —*Psalm 60:12*

WITH GOD WE SHALL DO VALIANTLY

When I recall my difficulties in 1989, I am in wonder at the countless ways I could have been harmed and silenced for all eternity. But that did not happen. Closed doors opened, obstacles evaporated, impossibilities dissipated, and I moved through a veritable war zone unscathed.

See also: Job 42:1–6

LET ME DWELL IN YOUR TENT FOREVER! LET ME TAKE REFUGE UNDER THE SHELTER OF YOUR WINGS! —*Psalm 61:4*

THE SHELTER OF YOUR WINGS

Jesus speaks of God's love for His children this way: "How often would I have gathered your children together as a hen gathers her brood under her wings but you were not willing." God offers us His protection. That is the given. The question is: Will we accept His offer?

See also: Matthew 23:37

FOR GOD ALONE MY SOUL WAITS IN SILENCE; FROM HIM COMES MY SALVATION. —*Psalm 62:1*

GOD IS MY SALVATION

Our faith can often be tested: "[His enemies] only plan to thrust him down from his high position. They take pleasure in falsehood. They bless with their mouths, but inwardly they curse." And yet the psalmist remains steadfast. God is his rock, his fortress, and his strength.

 See also: Psalm 62:2–4

FOR GOD ALONE, O MY SOUL, WAIT IN SILENCE, FOR MY HOPE IS FROM HIM. HE ONLY IS MY ROCK AND MY SALVATION, MY FORTRESS; I SHALL NOT BE SHAKEN. —*Psalm 62:5–6*

I SHALL NOT BE SHAKEN

The only good path to follow is built on the certainty that flows from genuine faith in God. Today, it seems, we have become codependent on the power of "science" to point the way forward, but in the hands of fallible people, that path can lead to disaster as well as promise.

See also: 1 Samuel 9:1–2, 1 Samuel 15:10–27

ONCE GOD HAS SPOKEN; TWICE HAVE I HEARD THIS: THAT POWER BELONGS TO GOD, AND THAT TO YOU, O LORD, BELONGS STEADFAST LOVE. FOR YOU WILL RENDER TO A MAN ACCORDING TO HIS WORK. —*Psalm 62:11–12*

THE WORK OF MAN

Every act has consequences. The cost of our decisions may not be clear at first, but over time, wrong decisions can overwhelm our best plans. When we rely, simply, on our own judgment, we should not be surprised if we find ourselves in the brambles and not where we intended to be.

See also: Genesis 4:4–7

YOU, GOD, ARE MY GOD, EARNESTLY I SEEK YOU; I THIRST FOR YOU, MY WHOLE BEING LONGS FOR YOU, IN A DRY AND PARCHED LAND WHERE THERE IS NO WATER. —*Psalm 63:1 (NIV)*

MY SOUL THIRSTS FOR GOD

Despite appearances, we do live in a parched land, and the water we seek is the Holy Spirit. To the woman at the well Jesus says, "whoever drinks the water I give them will never thirst. The water I give them will become in them a spring of water welling up to eternal life."

See also: John 4:7–26

BECAUSE YOUR STEADFAST LOVE IS BETTER THAN LIFE, MY LIPS WILL PRAISE YOU. —*Psalm 63:3*

BETTER THAN LIFE

God is better than life because God is unwavering, ready to enfold us in his embrace. He is near even when we behave like fugitives. We waver, hide, and lie to ourselves and others, but even then, God is reaching out and calling us to turn back to him. Will we ever stop fleeing?

See also: Luke 15:1–7

THE WHOLE EARTH IS FILLED WITH AWE AT YOUR WONDERS; WHERE MORNING DAWNS, WHERE EVENING FADES, YOU CALL FORTH SONGS OF JOY. —*Psalm 65:8 (NIV)*

YOUR WORKS, O GOD, ARE EVIDENT TO ALL

Behind the mystery, beauty, and wonder of creation is God himself. "For since the creation of the world God's invisible qualities—his eternal power and divine nature—have been clearly seen, being understood from what has been made, so that people are without excuse."

See also: Romans 1:19–20

YOU CROWN THE YEAR WITH YOUR BOUNTY, AND YOUR CARTS OVERFLOW WITH ABUNDANCE. THE GRASSLANDS OF THE WILDERNESS OVERFLOW; THE HILLS ARE CLOTHED WITH GLADNESS. —*Psalm 65:11,13 (NIV)*

ABUNDANCE

I feel a deep sense of joy when I read these verses. My imagination takes flight and I land in a summer setting surrounded by fields and trees with their leaves dancing to the rhythm of afternoon breeze. Soon I awaken from my revelry, but I know I have tasted a bit of Eden.

See also: Revelation 2:7

SHOUT FOR JOY TO GOD, ALL THE EARTH; SING THE GLORY OF HIS NAME; GIVE TO HIM GLORIOUS PRAISE! —*Psalm 66:1–2*

GIVE GOD GLORIOUS PRAISE

Deo Omnis Gloria! All glory to God! God is our life, our purpose, our path. When we glorify God with our lives, we are living in step with God's will for us. Jesus said, "Father, glorify me in your presence with the glory that I had with you before the world existed."

See also: John 17:1–10

COME AND SEE WHAT GOD HAS DONE: HE IS AWESOME IN HIS DEEDS TOWARD THE CHILDREN OF MAN. —*Psalm 66:5*

COME AND SEE

God is inviting us into His story: "Come and see." All are invited, but tragically, many find reasons to not accept God's call. They might say: My job or my family or a very important urgent errand must have my full attention. I suppose it boils down to priorities.

See also: Matthew 8:18–22

I CRIED TO (GOD) WITH MY MOUTH, AND HIGH PRAISE WAS ON MY TONGUE. IF I HAD CHERISHED INIQUITY IN MY HEART, THE LORD WOULD NOT HAVE LISTENED. BUT TRULY GOD HAS LISTENED; HE HAS ATTENDED TO THE VOICE OF MY PRAYER. *—Psalm 66:17–19*

COME AND HEAR

In the streets of the city we hear a cacophony of competing noises: horns blare, sirens scream, voices fight to be heard. But when God speaks, those noises fall away, and we hear the "sound of a low whisper." Something in our spirit knows that God is calling. Listen, and hear.

See also: 1 Kings 19:9–15

MAY GOD BE GRACIOUS TO US AND BLESS US AND MAKE HIS FACE TO SHINE UPON US, THAT YOUR WAY MAY BE KNOWN ON EARTH, YOUR SAVING POWER AMONG ALL NATIONS. —*Psalm 67:1–2*

MAY GOD BE GRACIOUS

What does it mean to be blessed by God? We can be blessed with family and well being and we want this, but sometimes when we have wandered away from God, he blesses us with adversities of many kinds to wake us up and bring us back to his purpose for us as he did with Jonah.

See also: Jonah 1:1–6

GOD SHALL ARISE, HIS ENEMIES SHALL BE SCATTERED; AND THOSE WHO HATE HIM SHALL FLEE BEFORE HIM! —*Psalm 68:1*

GOD SHALL ARISE

We often hear that we have been born for a purpose, but can that purpose be apart from God's will for us? At a spiritual crossroads moment in my own life, I responded to God's gentle whisper, and to my everlasting surprise, I turned to take the road God had planned for me all along.

See also: Jeremiah 6:16

SING TO GOD, SING PRAISES TO HIS NAME; LIFT UP A SONG TO HIM WHO
RIDES THROUGH THE DESERTS; HIS NAME IS THE LORD; EXULT BEFORE HIM!

—Psalm 68:4

SING TO GOD

Song expresses the beauty and mystery of God behind everything in the universe:
"The heavens declare the glory of God, and the sky above proclaims his handiwork."
Sing, therefore, "sing, O daughter of Zion, for behold, I come and I will dwell in
your midst, declares the Lord."

See also: Psalm 19:1, Zechariah 2:10

BLESSED BE THE LORD, WHO DAILY BEARS US UP; GOD IS OUR SALVATION.

—Psalm 68:19

GOD BEARS US UP

Jesus said "I can do nothing on my own." Nor can we. To believe otherwise is dangerously foolish. But believe in Jesus and you will begin to walk in step with God's purpose of restoration. "I can do all things through him who strengthens me."

See also: John 5:30, Philippians 4:13

O KINGDOMS OF THE EARTH, SING TO GOD; SING PRAISES TO THE LORD, TO HIM WHO RIDES IN THE HEAVENS, THE ANCIENT HEAVENS; BEHOLD, HE SENDS OUT HIS VOICE, HIS MIGHTY VOICE. —*Psalm 68:32–33*

GOD'S MIGHTY VOICE

God's mighty voice can come as a "low whisper" to Elijah or to the disciples in an upper room as a mighty rushing wind filling the entire room or as the sound of a trumpet. God does not speak only in one way, but he does speak to one purpose.

See also: 1 Corinthians 2:12–13, Colossians 3:16

SAVE ME, O GOD! FOR THE WATERS HAVE COME UP TO MY NECK. I SINK IN DEEP MIRE, WHERE THERE IS NO FOOTHOLD; I HAVE COME INTO DEEP WATERS, AND THE FLOOD SWEEPS OVER ME. —*Psalm 69:1–2*

I SINK IN DEEP MIRE

It would be easy to discount prayer in our lives, especially when everything is as we would like it. But when the turbulent waters are rising; when our foothold slips and we are sinking in the miry deep, what are we to do? Jesus prayed to the Father continuously. He is our model.

See also: Matthew 14:23, Psalm 19:3–18

O GOD, YOU KNOW MY FOLLY; THE WRONGS I HAVE DONE ARE NOT HIDDEN FROM YOU. —*Psalm 69:5*

NOTHING IS HIDDEN FROM YOU

Given our inclination to wander, it might seem comforting to think our folly and our wrongs are hidden from God, but to believe our waywardness is invisible to him is to compound our wrongs by dismissing God's power to see and know everything. Nothing is hidden from God.

See also: Luke 8:16–18

FOR ZEAL FOR YOUR HOUSE HAS CONSUMED ME, AND THE REPROACHES OF THOSE WHO REPROACH YOU HAVE FALLEN ON ME. —*Psalm 69:9*

ZEAL

Jesus goes to Jerusalem and finds the Temple has been overrun by "money–changers." He cannot accept that the "things of this world" would be permitted to invade the sacred Temple; And his disciples remember the words of the psalm: "Zeal for your house will consume me."

See also: John 2:17

BUT AS FOR ME, MY PRAYER IS TO YOU, O LORD. AT AN ACCEPTABLE TIME, O GOD, IN THE ABUNDANCE OF YOUR STEADFAST LOVE ANSWER ME IN YOUR SAVING FAITHFULNESS. —*Psalm 69:13*

ANSWER ME LORD

Job experiences one of our great fears: That our world will be turned upside down, that we will lose everything, and that all goodness and health will flee from us. All of this happens to Job and yet he doesn't turn on his Creator: "Though he slay me, I will hope in him."

See also: Job 13:15, Psalm 34:4

MAKE HASTE, O GOD, TO DELIVER ME! O LORD, MAKE HASTE TO HELP ME!

—Psalm 70:1

MAKE HASTE, O GOD

Everything is spinning faster: Emails are marked urgent; meetings are urgent; people walk the sidewalks urgently typing in messages to a hoped for connection and to what end? In the meantime, everything progresses on God's own time. Slow down. God will provide what is needed.

See also: Psalm 37:34

MAY ALL WHO SEEK YOU REJOICE AND BE GLAD IN YOU! MAY THOSE WHO LOVE YOUR SALVATION SAY EVERMORE, "GOD IS GREAT!" —*Psalm 70:4*

GOD IS GREAT!

To say that God is great is to say that God is mighty and merciful; he is love; he is our refuge, our strength, our salvation; he is faithful, true, good, holy, and near; he is light and so much more than can be described here or anywhere.

See also: Nehemiah 8:10

IN YOUR RIGHTEOUSNESS DELIVER ME AND RESCUE ME; INCLINE YOUR EAR TO ME, AND SAVE ME! —*Psalm 71:2*

LORD, INCLINE YOUR EAR TO ME

In Gethsemane, Jesus knows what lies ahead: "My soul is very sorrowful, even to death." He also knows his Father's will and what this hour means: "My Father, if it is possible, let this cup pass from me; nevertheless, not as I will, but as you will." The Lord is his strength...and ours.

See also: Matthew 26:39

FOR YOU, O LORD, ARE MY HOPE, MY TRUST, O LORD, FROM MY YOUTH.
UPON YOU I HAVE LEANED FROM BEFORE MY BIRTH; YOU ARE HE WHO
TOOK ME FROM MY MOTHER'S WOMB. MY PRAISE IS CONTINUALLY OF YOU.

—Psalm 71:5–6

YOU ARE MY HOPE

Think of the disciples in Gethsemane and then put yourself there beside them. The triumphant entry is now only a memory. Their hope has been taken prisoner and they have fled in fear for their lives. Place yourself there. What could we have done? What would we have done?

See also: Matthew 26:47–56

DO NOT CAST ME OFF IN THE TIME OF OLD AGE; FORSAKE ME NOT WHEN MY STRENGTH IS SPENT. —*Psalm 71:9*

REMAIN WITH ME, O LORD

Our faithfulness and effectiveness on behalf of the Lord should never be limited by age: "Now Moses was eighty years old, and Aaron eighty–three years old, when they spoke to Pharaoh." Pray you will be blessed with strength to serve God everyday for all of your days.

See also: Exodus 7:7

O GOD, BE NOT FAR FROM ME; O MY GOD, MAKE HASTE TO HELP ME!

—Psalm 71:12

GOD ANSWERS PRAYER

When life is prosperous and good, the inclination is to inflate our own virtues as the cause for our good fortune. But reverse everything, as happened to Job, and what will we then do? I reached out to God. I called for help. He is near. He can hear you and will open doors.

See also: 1 Kings 19:1–8

SO EVEN TO OLD AGE AND GRAY HAIRS, O GOD, DO NOT FORSAKE ME, UNTIL I PROCLAIM YOUR MIGHT TO ANOTHER GENERATION, YOUR POWER TO ALL THOSE TO COME. —*Psalm 71:18*

I WILL PROCLAIM YOU, LORD

To follow Jesus is a call to action now. "Remember also your Creator in the days of your youth, before the evil days come and the years draw near of which you will say, 'I have no pleasure in them'; before the silver cord is snapped…and the spirit returns to God who gave it."

See also: Ecclesiastes 12:1–8

YOUR RIGHTEOUSNESS, O GOD, REACHES THE HIGH HEAVENS. YOU WHO HAVE DONE GREAT THINGS, O GOD, WHO IS LIKE YOU? YOU WHO HAVE MADE ME SEE MANY TROUBLES AND CALAMITIES WILL REVIVE ME AGAIN; FROM THE DEPTHS OF THE EARTH YOU WILL BRING ME UP AGAIN. —*Psalm 71:19–20*

GOD, WHO IS LIKE YOU?

There is no god like our God. Moses said to Pharaoh, "Be it as you say, so that you know that there is no one like the Lord our God." What about us? Peter, quoting scripture, says be holy because God is holy; all the more reason to know Jesus and follow him always.

See also: 1 John 1:7

MY LIPS WILL SHOUT FOR JOY, WHEN I SING PRAISES TO YOU; MY SOUL ALSO, WHICH YOU HAVE REDEEMED. —*Psalm 71:23*

MY SOUL SHOUTS FOR JOY

Joy is a fruit of the Holy Spirit. Joy is not happiness. Happiness is a passing condition. We yearn for it, it arrives, and then it soon vanishes. Joy is an overflowing in our heart when we draw close to the goodness and beauty of our Creator. It is a taste of eternity.

See also: Galatians 5:22

LET THE MOUNTAINS BEAR PROSPERITY FOR THE PEOPLE, AND THE HILLS, IN RIGHTEOUSNESS! MAY HE DEFEND THE CAUSE OF THE POOR OF THE PEOPLE, GIVE DELIVERANCE TO THE CHILDREN OF THE NEEDY, AND CRUSH THE OPPRESSOR! —*Psalm 72:3–4*

DEFEND US, O LORD

The 2nd Psalm says the rulers of earth are at war with God. "The kings of the earth set themselves, and the rulers take counsel together, against his Anointed." Whether it was Herod, or the Pharisees or the crowds of people of Jerusalem, many wanted Jesus condemned and eliminated.

   See also: Psalm 2:1–3, John 3:35–36

MAY HE BE LIKE RAIN THAT FALLS ON THE MOWN GRASS, LIKE SHOWERS THAT WATER THE EARTH! —*Psalm 72:6*

A RIGHTEOUS KING

There are kings and then there are righteous kings: "When one rules justly over men, ruling in the fear of God, he dawns on them like the morning light, like the sun shining forth on a cloudless morning, like rain that makes the grass spout from the earth."

See also: Samuel 23:3–4

BLESSED BE THE LORD, THE GOD OF ISRAEL, WHO ALONE DOES WONDROUS THINGS. BLESSED BE HIS GLORIOUS NAME FOREVER; MAY THE WHOLE EARTH BE FILLED WITH HIS GLORY! AMEN AND AMEN! —*Psalm 72:18–19*

BLESSED BE THE LORD

Many believe in miracles, but have a tough time attributing them to the God of the Bible. The god they seem to prefer inhabit a small bit of real estate south of San Francisco. The god's name is Silicon and he lives in a valley and he makes billionaires out of mere mortals.

See also: Isaiah 44:17

BUT AS FOR ME, MY FEET HAD ALMOST STUMBLED, MY STEPS HAD NEARLY SLIPPED. FOR I WAS ENVIOUS OF THE ARROGANT WHEN I SAW THE PROSPERITY OF THE WICKED. —*Psalm 73:2–3*

ENVY

The psalmist almost stumbled out of envy of others. Jesus says envy defiles the heart. Paul says that love does not envy or boast and the author of Proverbs says envy "makes the bones rot." Envy is a sin and a deadly one at that. To envy means we are out of sorts with God.

See also: *Mark 7:20–23, 1 Corinthians 13:4, Proverbs 14:30*

YOU GUIDE ME WITH YOUR COUNSEL, AND AFTERWARD YOU WILL RECEIVE ME TO GLORY. WHOM HAVE I IN HEAVEN BUT YOU? AND THERE IS NOTHING ON EARTH THAT I DESIRE BESIDES YOU. —*Psalm 73:24–25*

YOU GUIDE ME

God did not come to Elijah in a strong wind, nor in an earthquake, nor in a fire. He came to Elijah as the "the sound of a quiet whisper." How can we be guided by God's counsel if we have blocked our ears to the point of not hearing God's quiet, gentle voice?

See also: 1 Kings 19:11–12

MY FLESH AND MY HEART MAY FAIL, BUT GOD IS THE STRENGTH OF MY HEART AND MY PORTION FOREVER. —*Psalm 73:26*

MY FLESH WILL FAIL

What strengthened the hearts of the disciples after the crucifixion? The weight of the world has crashed down, leaving them emptied of hope. And then the sun rose and everything changed and they realized Jesus was alive! "The Lord has risen!" The Lord has overcome death!

See also: Mark 16:1–8

BUT FOR ME IT IS GOOD TO BE NEAR GOD; I HAVE MADE THE LORD GOD MY REFUGE, THAT I MAY TELL OF ALL YOUR WORKS. —*Psalm 73:28*

THE LORD IS NEAR

In Athens, Paul found that many were religious, but the gods they believed in were mere projections of human nature writ large. Paul tells them of a God who came to earth to walk amongst mortals and who died on a cross to rise from the dead and is alive and near. And he has a name.

　　　　　　See also: Jeremiah 23:23–24, Acts 17:22–34

LET NOT THE DOWNTRODDEN TURN BACK IN SHAME; LET THE POOR AND NEEDY PRAISE YOUR NAME. ARISE, O GOD, DEFEND YOUR CAUSE; REMEMBER HOW THE FOOLISH SCOFF AT YOU ALL THE DAY! —*Psalm 74:21–22*

ARISE, O GOD

"The foolish scoff at you all the day," says the psalmist. Why? "For the fool speaks folly, and his heart is busy with iniquity, to practice ungodliness, to utter error concerning the Lord, to leave the craving of the hungry unsatisfied, and to deprive the thirsty of drink."

See also: Isaiah 32:6

"AT THE SET TIME THAT I APPOINT I WILL JUDGE WITH EQUITY. WHEN THE EARTH TOTTERS, AND ALL ITS INHABITANTS, IT IS I WHO KEEP STEADY ITS PILLARS." —*Psalm 75:2–3*

GOD WILL JUDGE WITH EQUITY

Where can true justice be found? Can we look to political figures? Stalin in the 1930s used the justice system to condemn his enemies; Hitler did the same. Both men posed as symbols of a new human religion. They were killers with the power to kill. They were devils, not gods.

See also: John 8:39–47

FROM THE HEAVENS YOU UTTERED JUDGMENT; THE EARTH FEARED AND WAS STILL, WHEN GOD AROSE TO ESTABLISH JUDGMENT, TO SAVE ALL THE HUMBLE OF THE EARTH. —*Psalm 76:8– 9*

THE WISDOM OF GOD/THE WISDOM OF MAN

Solomon displayed great wisdom when he asked the Lord not for riches or long life, but for a discerning heart: "Give your servant an understanding mind to govern your people, that I may discern between good and evil, for who is able to govern this your people?" Who indeed?

See also: 1 Kings 3:9

MAKE YOUR VOWS TO THE LORD YOUR GOD AND PERFORM THEM; LET ALL AROUND HIM BRING GIFTS TO HIM WHO IS TO BE FEARED, WHO CUTS OFF THE SPIRIT OF PRINCES, WHO IS TO BE FEARED BY THE KINGS OF THE EARTH. —*Psalm 76:11–12*

MAKE YOUR VOWS TO THE LORD

Vows are a promise. In the Sermon on the Mount, Jesus says, "All you need to say is simply 'Yes' or 'No'; anything beyond this comes from the evil one." Why? Because when you swear and don't mean it, you are lying. And one lie can put anyone on a very crooked and tortuous path.

See also: Matthew 5:37

THEN I SAID, "I WILL APPEAL TO THIS, TO THE YEARS OF THE RIGHT HAND OF THE MOST HIGH." I WILL REMEMBER THE DEEDS OF THE LORD; YES, I WILL REMEMBER YOUR WONDERS OF OLD. —*Psalm 77:10–11*

YOUR WONDERS OF OLD

When we shackle everyday life to the intense present, we can become like swirling vapors, aimlessly wandering here and there without an anchor or compass. The "wonders of old" are evidence of God operating in this world: He wants us to believe and join forces with him.

See also: Isaiah 25:1

I WILL PONDER ALL YOUR WORK, AND MEDITATE ON YOUR MIGHTY DEEDS.

—Psalm 77:12

YOUR MIGHTY DEEDS

To acknowledge that we have a God and that we are not our own god represents a huge step from the self–centered life into a God–centered life. Often a crisis will precipitate this change of heart and mind. And this new God–centered focus will set the course for future action.

See also: Acts 9:1–9

YOUR WAY, O GOD, IS HOLY. WHAT GOD IS GREAT LIKE OUR GOD?

—Psalm 77:13

YOUR WAY, O GOD, IS HOLY

Holiness has two aspects: God is holy and we are not. While we can never obtain the holiness of God, we can respond to the same offer Jesus extended to the rich young ruler: "come, and follow me." He declined the offer in favor of what he had. As for us, the offer remains open.

See also: Luke 18:22

GIVE EAR, O MY PEOPLE, TO MY TEACHING; INCLINE YOUR EARS TO THE WORDS OF MY MOUTH! I WILL OPEN MY MOUTH IN A PARABLE; I WILL UTTER DARK SAYINGS FROM OF OLD, THINGS THAT WE HAVE HEARD AND KNOWN, THAT OUR FATHERS HAVE TOLD US. —*Psalm 78:1–3*

TELL THE NEXT GENERATION

From almost right after a baby is born, our teaching role gets underway. Just holding our baby close to our beating heart teaches implicitly the power of love. And over time we begin to tell about the God who created the skies, the mountains, the seas, and you and me.

See also: Luke 2:1–7

THEREFORE, WHEN THE LORD HEARD, HE WAS FULL OF WRATH; A FIRE WAS KINDLED AGAINST JACOB; HIS ANGER ROSE AGAINST ISRAEL, BECAUSE THEY DID NOT BELIEVE IN GOD AND DID NOT TRUST HIS SAVING POWER.

—Psalm 78:21–22

HE DID NOT BELIEVE IN GOD

We hear of God but we live for ourselves. We say with the Rich Fool, "Soul, you have ample goods laid up for many years; relax, eat, drink, be merry. But God said to him, 'Fool! This night your soul is required of you, and the things you have prepared, whose will they be?'"

IN SPITE OF ALL THIS, THEY STILL SINNED; DESPITE HIS WONDERS, THEY DID NOT BELIEVE. SO HE MADE THEIR DAYS VANISH LIKE A BREATH, AND THEIR YEARS IN TERROR. —*Psalm 78:32–33*

THEIR DAYS VANISHED

Jesus died so that we might live. Without reconciliation with God, there is no salvation. Jesus is the lamb who goes to his death in our place: "Be reconciled to God. For our sake he made him to be sin who knew no sin, so that in him we might become the righteousness of God."

See also: 2 Corinthians 5:20–21

THEIR HEART WAS NOT STEADFAST TOWARD HIM; THEY WERE NOT FAITHFUL TO HIS COVENANT. —*Psalm 78:37*

TO BE FAITHFUL

After the resurrection, Jesus asks Peter three times, "Simon, son of John, do you love me?" Just a few days earlier, Peter had denied knowing Jesus. Out of fear he had failed the Lord completely. Jesus knows that it is only complete devotion to the Lord that will drive out fear.

See also: John 21:15–19

YET HE, BEING COMPASSIONATE, ATONED FOR THEIR INIQUITY AND DID NOT DESTROY THEM; HE RESTRAINED HIS ANGER OFTEN AND DID NOT STIR UP ALL HIS WRATH. HE REMEMBERED THAT THEY WERE BUT FLESH, A WIND THAT PASSES AND COMES NOT AGAIN —*Psalm 78:38–39*

A WIND THAT PASSES

The Bible often reminds us that our time here on earth is fleeting, much like the springtime flowers of the fields: "You sweep them away as with a flood; they are like a dream, in the morning it flourishes and is renewed; in the evening it fades and withers."

See also: Psalm 90:6

O GOD, THE NATIONS HAVE COME INTO YOUR INHERITANCE; THEY HAVE DEFILED YOUR HOLY TEMPLE; THEY HAVE LAID JERUSALEM IN RUINS.

—Psalm 79:1

JERUSALEM LAID WASTE

Over 2,600 years ago Jerusalem was under siege by an invading army. Soon David's city would fall with many of the people forced into exile. Jeremiah warned the leaders that God would not be mocked by their indifference and corruption. He would "make void their plans."

See also: Jeremiah 19:7

THEY HAVE GIVEN THE BODIES OF YOUR SERVANTS TO THE BIRDS OF THE HEAVENS FOR FOOD, THE FLESH OF YOUR FAITHFUL TO THE BEASTS OF THE EARTH. —*Psalm 79:2*

DESOLATION

David's city was fortified to withstand attacking armies. But there was not provision for the rot within: "For the sons of Judah have done evil in my sight," declares the Lord. "They have set their detestable things in the house that is called by my name."

See also: Jeremiah 7:30

THEY HAVE POURED OUT THEIR BLOOD LIKE WATER ALL AROUND
JERUSALEM, AND THERE WAS NO ONE TO BURY THEM. —*Psalm 79:3*

NO ONE LEFT

The devastation of Jerusalem is complete; the walls are down, the Temple destroyed and the people dying: "In the dust of the streets lie the young and the old; my young women and my young men have fallen by the sword..."

WHY SHOULD THE NATIONS SAY, "WHERE IS THEIR GOD?" LET THE AVENGING OF THE OUTPOURED BLOOD OF YOUR SERVANTS BE KNOWN AMONG THE NATIONS BEFORE OUR EYES! LET THE GROANS OF THE PRISONERS COME BEFORE YOU.... —*Psalm 79:10–11*

" W H E R E   I S   T H E I R   G O D ? "

The question is not "why has God abandoned us?" It is "Why have we abandoned God?" The priests and the prophets lied and the people believed them: Jeremiah said, "Do not listen to the words of the prophets...for it is a lie that they are prophesying to you."

See also: Jeremiah 27:14

BUT WE YOUR PEOPLE, THE SHEEP OF YOUR PASTURE, WILL GIVE THANKS TO YOU FOREVER; FROM GENERATION TO GENERATION WE WILL RECOUNT YOUR PRAISE. —*Psalm 79:13*

WE WILL RECOUNT YOUR PRAISE

What happens if we fail to recount "God's grace" to the next generation? Surely we will lapse into a godless culture leading to one focused on "bread and circuses." And what will follow from that is a return to a world where God's way and our way run on different tracks.

See also: Isaiah 55:8

RESTORE US, O GOD; LET YOUR FACE SHINE, THAT WE MAY BE SAVED!

—Psalm 80:3

RESTORE US, O GOD

When Paradise was lost, our ancient ancestors awoke in a place that, while beautiful, was pitiless and severe. They found themselves at war with each other and with God. Conflict and death became part of the human story, but not the only part, for God himself is the ultimate narrator.

See also: Genesis 3:22–24

IN DISTRESS YOU CALLED, AND I DELIVERED YOU; I ANSWERED YOU IN THE
SECRET PLACE OF THUNDER; I TESTED YOU AT THE WATERS OF MERIBAH.

—Psalm 81:7

IN DISTRESS, YOU CALLED ME

The Bible tells the story of God's desire to free us from the sin that binds. In
Exodus, He intervenes through Moses to unshackle his people from slavery. This act
foreshadows Golgotha where the Son of God dies as a substitute for us so that we
might live free from the sin that has separated us from Him.

See also: Exodus 3:1–22

ARISE, O GOD, JUDGE THE EARTH; FOR YOU SHALL INHERIT ALL THE NATIONS! —*Psalm 82:8*

JUDGE THE EARTH, O GOD

The psalmist prophesizes that God will "inherit all the nations." Jesus prays that God's Kingdom will come," but right now "the nations rage and the peoples plot in vain." He warns the world will resist; it will hate you as it hated me.

See also: Matthew 6:10, Psalm 2:1, John 17:14

HOW LOVELY IS YOUR DWELLING PLACE, O LORD OF HOSTS! MY SOUL LONGS, YES, FAINTS FOR THE COURTS OF THE LORD; MY HEART AND FLESH SING FOR JOY TO THE LIVING GOD. —*Psalm 84:1–2*

I SING FOR JOY TO THE LIVING GOD

The things of this world can be good, but they are really a mere copy and a shadow of the goodness, holiness, and greatness of God. When we accept this truth in faith, then with our whole being we will manifest our delight through living a life infused with the Holy Spirit.

See also: Galatians 5:22–23

BLESSED ARE THOSE WHO DWELL IN YOUR HOUSE, EVER SINGING YOUR PRAISE! —*Psalm 84:4*

EVER SINGING YOUR PRAISE

Music is the heart of worship: "Be filled with the Spirit, addressing one another in psalms and hymns and spiritual songs, singing and making melody to the Lord with your heart, giving thanks always and for everything to God the Father, in the name of our Lord Jesus Christ."

See also: Ephesians 5:18–20

BEHOLD OUR SHIELD, O GOD; LOOK ON THE FACE OF YOUR ANOINTED!
FOR A DAY IN YOUR COURTS IS BETTER THAN A THOUSAND ELSEWHERE.
I WOULD RATHER BE A DOORKEEPER IN THE HOUSE OF MY GOD THAN
DWELL IN THE TENTS OF WICKEDNESS. —*Psalm 84:9–10*

THE TENTS OF THE WICKED

The reality of "wickedness" has been replaced with an all–purpose inclusiveness. The thief is a needy fellow, the murderer has a grievance, and the prostitute's heart is gold. We are at a point of justifying sin, even within the church, in the name of "niceness." When this happens, trouble begins to brew.

See also: Romans 1:18–32

FOR THE LORD GOD IS A SUN AND SHIELD; THE LORD BESTOWS FAVOR AND HONOR. NO GOOD THING DOES HE WITHHOLD FROM THOSE WHO WALK UPRIGHTLY. O LORD OF HOSTS, BLESSED IS THE ONE WHO TRUSTS IN YOU!

—Psalm 84:11–12

TRUST IN GOD

Trust is a necessary component of living. But not everyone is trustworthy. We often learn this truth the hard way. It is good to remember this: "It is better to take refuge in the Lord than to trust in man. It is better to take refuge in the Lord than to trust in princes."

See also: Psalm 118:8–9

LORD, YOU WERE FAVORABLE TO YOUR LAND; YOU RESTORED THE
FORTUNES OF JACOB. YOU FORGAVE THE INIQUITY OF YOUR PEOPLE; YOU
COVERED ALL THEIR SIN. —*Psalm 85:1–2*

YOU COVERED ALL THEIR SIN

If you are haunted by old conflicts and transgressions, then you are living a life
where your sins fester and never go away. You come to believe this burden cannot
be removed and so you suffer with it. All of us need the forgiveness that is found at
the foot of the cross.

See also: Ephesians 4:32

RESTORE US AGAIN, O GOD OF OUR SALVATION, AND PUT AWAY YOUR INDIGNATION TOWARD US! —*Psalm 85:4*

RESTORE US

The psalmist is pleading with God to restore the people of Israel, the chosen nation God had set apart for his purposes. But when Jesus begins his ministry on earth, he moves the focus away from the nation and to the individual. He says to us time and again, "repent and believe."

See also: Psalm 1:5-6, 1 John 3:4-7

SHOW US YOUR STEADFAST LOVE, O LORD, AND GRANT US YOUR SALVATION.

—Psalm 85:7

GOD'S STEADFAST LOVE

We are blessed when we know that "there is no fear in love, but perfect love casts out all fear. For fear has to do with punishment, and whoever fears has not been perfected in love." Living in faith in our Lord Jesus Christ is to live with a joyful spirit and not one of fear.

See also: 1 John 4:18

LET ME HEAR WHAT GOD THE LORD WILL SPEAK, FOR HE WILL SPEAK PEACE TO HIS PEOPLE, TO HIS SAINTS; BUT LET THEM NOT TURN BACK TO FOLLY. —*Psalm 85:8*

GLORIFY GOD WITH YOUR LIFE

God is asking something of you and me and here is part of it in a nutshell: "To fear the Lord your God, to walk in his ways, to love him, to serve the Lord your God with all your heart and with all your soul, and to keep the commandments of the Lord."

See also: Deuteronomy 10:12–13

SURELY HIS SALVATION IS NEAR TO THOSE WHO FEAR HIM, THAT GLORY MAY DWELL IN OUR LAND. —*Psalm 85:9*

SALVATION IS NEAR

At times it is possible to think God is indifferent to our plight. Job's suffering leads him to cry out, "What is man, that you make so much of him, and that you set your heart on him, visit him every morning and test him every moment?" It is only later that Job sees the truth.

See also: Job 7:17–18

YES, THE LORD WILL GIVE WHAT IS GOOD, AND OUR LAND WILL YIELD ITS INCREASE. RIGHTEOUSNESS WILL GO BEFORE HIM AND MAKE HIS FOOTSTEPS A WAY. —*Psalm 85:12–13*

THE RIGHTEOUS PATH

Jesus is the Good Shepherd who will "tend his flock; he will gather the lambs into his arms; he will carry them in his bosom, and gently lead those that are with young."

See also: Isaiah 40:11

INCLINE YOUR EAR, O LORD, AND ANSWER ME, FOR I AM POOR AND NEEDY. PRESERVE MY LIFE, FOR I AM GODLY; SAVE YOUR SERVANT, WHO TRUSTS IN YOU—YOU ARE MY GOD. —*Psalm 86:1–2*

PRESERVE MY LIFE, O LORD

Prayer is an ongoing conversation with God. When things are rough, it is easy to raise our internal voice, but remember God is not hard of hearing. We must keep the conversation going, even if the answer is not instantly given. Pray continuously. Trust always.

See also: Ephesians 6:16–20

GIVE EAR, O LORD, TO MY PRAYER; LISTEN TO MY PLEA FOR GRACE.

—Psalm 86:6

LISTEN TO MY PLEA

The psalmist affirms the character of God. God's overwhelming desire to forgive and restore is built on the foundation of his love. Grace is a gift of God available to all, if only we will turn, believe, and accept.

See also: 1 John 4:7–16

IN THE DAY OF MY TROUBLE I CALL UPON YOU, FOR YOU ANSWER ME.

—Psalm 86:7

YOU ANSWER ME

Prayer is a way of life, not just a last resort. We should be in prayer ceaselessly, but unfortunately we too often revert to earthbound reasoning in navigating through everyday events instead of "praying at all times in the Spirit."

See also: Ephesians 6:18

ALL THE NATIONS YOU HAVE MADE SHALL COME AND WORSHIP BEFORE YOU, O LORD, AND SHALL GLORIFY YOUR NAME. —*Psalm 86:9*

ALL GLORY TO GOD

The restoration of God's Kingdom is promised to be fulfilled in God's time. Jesus prophesied that our world would remain at war with the Father: "And you will hear of wars and rumors of wars. See that you are not alarmed, for this must take place, but the end is not yet."

See also: Matthew 24:8

TEACH ME YOUR WAY, O LORD, THAT I MAY WALK IN YOUR TRUTH; UNITE MY HEART TO FEAR YOUR NAME. I GIVE THANKS TO YOU, O LORD MY GOD, WITH MY WHOLE HEART, AND I WILL GLORIFY YOUR NAME FOREVER.

—Psalm 86:11–12

TEACH ME YOUR WAY

There is grave danger when church leaders wander away from biblical truth: "For a time is coming when people will not endure sound teaching, but having itching ears they will accumulate for themselves teachers to suit their own passions and will turn away from listening to the truth and wander off into myths."

See also: 2 Timothy 4:3–4

BUT YOU, O LORD, ARE A GOD MERCIFUL AND GRACIOUS, SLOW TO ANGER AND ABOUNDING IN STEADFAST LOVE AND FAITHFULNESS. —*Psalm 86:15*

YOU, O GOD, ARE MERCIFUL AND GRACIOUS

When we inflate our own importance in the greater scheme of things, we simultaneously deflate God in every way. Alexander Pope, the 18th Century poet, reflected this modernist conceit when he wrote, "The proper study of Mankind is Man." In such a world, self regard becomes everything.

See also: 2 Timothy 3:2–5

ON THE HOLY MOUNT STANDS THE CITY HE FOUNDED; THE LORD LOVES THE GATES OF ZION MORE THAN ALL THE DWELLING PLACES OF JACOB. GLORIOUS THINGS OF YOU ARE SPOKEN, O CITY OF GOD. —*Psalm 87:1–3*

THE CITY OF GOD

To David and his heirs, Jerusalem was the "City of God." It was built on a hill with the wild desert on one side and the sea far off on the other. Over time, though, David's heirs forgot God. This place, built to glorify God, steadily descended into merely a "City of Man."

See also: Psalm 122

O LORD, GOD OF MY SALVATION, I CRY OUT DAY AND NIGHT BEFORE YOU.

LET MY PRAYER COME BEFORE YOU; INCLINE YOUR EAR TO MY CRY!

—Psalm 88:1–2

I CRY OUT

In Jerusalem I visited Caiphas' house. When Jesus was taken prisoner, he was marched to this place where he was shackled and beaten. We stood on the steps of the dungeon and read this psalm. As the words echoed off the stone walls, we felt we could hear Jesus uttering these words.

See also: Psalm 88

BUT I, O LORD, CRY TO YOU; IN THE MORNING MY PRAYER COMES BEFORE YOU. O LORD, WHY DO YOU CAST MY SOUL AWAY? WHY DO YOU HIDE YOUR FACE FROM ME? —*Psalm 88:13–14*

WILL YOU ANSWER ME, O LORD

The atheist hangs his hat on the absence of God. He scans the heavens on a starry night and sees...nothing. He starts in denial and argues all the way down to the empty bottom of a black hole. Images of beauty and majesty do not stir him to awe. He is trapped in a conclusion.

See also: Psalm 14

I WILL SING OF THE STEADFAST LOVE OF THE LORD, FOREVER; WITH MY MOUTH I WILL MAKE KNOWN YOUR FAITHFULNESS TO ALL GENERATIONS.

—Psalm 89:1

GOD'S FAITHFULNESS

What will we be remembered for? It sometimes seems we live in a time of discardable stuff. Worse, we may have lost contact with the touchstones of the past that help us locate coherence and purpose in a well-ordered life. The psalmist sings because he sees God at work in everything.

See also: 1 Corinthians 14:15

YOU HAVE SAID, "I HAVE MADE A COVENANT WITH MY CHOSEN ONE; I HAVE SWORN TO DAVID MY SERVANT: 'I WILL ESTABLISH YOUR OFFSPRING FOREVER, AND BUILD YOUR THRONE FOR ALL GENERATIONS.'" —*Psalm 89:3–4*

GOD'S OATH TO DAVID

Jesus is God's promise fulfilled. The promise or oath can be found in the second book of Samuel. Through Nathan, God says of David, "I will raise up your offspring after you...and I will establish his kingdom." And "I will be to him a father and he to me shall be a son."

See also: 2 Samuel 7:8–16, Psalm 89:35–37

RIGHTEOUSNESS AND JUSTICE ARE THE FOUNDATION OF YOUR THRONE;
STEADFAST LOVE AND FAITHFULNESS GO BEFORE YOU. *—Psalm 89:14*

RIGHTEOUSNESS AND JUSTICE

This Kingdom will be built with the pillars of "righteousness and justice" and the King will be blessed forever. Those of the kingdom will show steadfast love and faithfulness for their Lord who will "ride out victoriously for the cause of truth and meekness and righteousness."

See also: Psalm 45:4

HE SHALL CRY TO ME, 'YOU ARE MY FATHER, MY GOD, AND THE ROCK OF MY SALVATION.' —*Psalm 89:26*

"THE HIGHEST OF THE KINGS OF THE EARTH"

The Lord's Prayer is a series of requests addressed to God. The first request is "thy kingdom come." This is the kingdom that will be but is not yet. This kingdom begins with the anointing of David and will lead a thousand years later to a child born to be the King of Kings.

See also: Matthew 6:5–15

ONCE FOR ALL I HAVE SWORN BY MY HOLINESS; I WILL NOT LIE TO DAVID. HIS OFFSPRING SHALL ENDURE FOREVER, HIS THRONE AS LONG AS THE SUN BEFORE ME. LIKE THE MOON IT SHALL BE ESTABLISHED FOREVER, A FAITHFUL WITNESS IN THE SKIES." —*Psalm 89:35–37*

DAVID'S THRONE

Peter and the disciples knew of God's promise to King David and they believed Jesus had come to earth to fulfill God's promise. But they also expected that Jesus, like David, would be a warrior king; they were not prepared at first for the Suffering Servant prophesied by Isaiah.

See also: Isaiah 53:1–12

YOU HAVE MADE HIS SPLENDOR TO CEASE AND CAST HIS THRONE TO THE GROUND. YOU HAVE CUT SHORT THE DAYS OF HIS YOUTH; YOU HAVE COVERED HIM WITH SHAME. HOW LONG, O LORD? WILL YOU HIDE YOURSELF FOREVER? HOW LONG WILL YOUR WRATH BURN LIKE FIRE? —*Psalm 89:44–46*

HIS SPLENDOR HAS CEASED

The psalmist recalls the splendor of David's Jerusalem; he remembers the promise that God would not forsake David. But Jerusalem is in ruins; the people have gone into exile and the Temple is destroyed. He cries out, "How long, O Lord?" Is the promise of restoration in ruins too?

See also: Lamentations 1:1–12

REMEMBER HOW SHORT MY TIME IS! FOR WHAT VANITY YOU HAVE CREATED ALL THE CHILDREN OF MAN! WHAT MAN CAN LIVE AND NEVER SEE DEATH? WHO CAN DELIVER HIS SOUL FROM THE POWER OF SHEOL? —*Psalm 89:47–48*

WAITING

There comes a time when hope is tested to the extreme. The psalmist's time is short; he may not live to see his dreams of restoration fulfilled. He says, "How long, O Lord? Will you hide yourself forever? How long will your wrath burn like fire?"

See also: Job 7:1–10

LORD, YOU HAVE BEEN OUR DWELLING PLACE IN ALL GENERATIONS. BEFORE THE MOUNTAINS WERE BROUGHT FORTH, OR EVER YOU HAD FORMED THE EARTH AND THE WORLD, FROM EVERLASTING TO EVERLASTING YOU ARE GOD. —*Psalm 90:1–2*

FROM EVERLASTING TO EVERLASTING

Our idea of time is earthbound. Time mirrors the astonishing precision of natural events such as the daily revolution of the earth. But in Genesis, we learn that the "beginning" is not the beginning; God exists before time as we know it; in creating heaven and earth, he also created time.

See also: Colossians 1:15–23

FOR A THOUSAND YEARS IN YOUR SIGHT ARE BUT AS YESTERDAY WHEN IT IS PAST, OR AS A WATCH IN THE NIGHT. —*Psalm 90:4*

GOD'S TIME

Each day contains the same amount of time. Depending on mood and circumstance, time seems to move at different speeds. For a child, time can creep, but for a busy adult, time flies away with the wind. And time past is strangest of all because it contracts into almost nothing.

See also: Ecclesiastes 12:1–8

YOU SWEEP THEM AWAY AS WITH A FLOOD; THEY ARE LIKE A DREAM, LIKE GRASS THAT IS RENEWED IN THE MORNING: IN THE MORNING IT FLOURISHES AND IS RENEWED; IN THE EVENING IT FADES AND WITHERS. —*Psalm 90:5–6*

LIKE A DREAM

Make believe is to wish for something to be true. We might wish that the good things in life would never go away but that is not the world we were born into. The psalmist turns to God and says though our years are short, please teach us "to number our days that we may get a heart of wisdom."

See also: Psalm 102:3–6, Psalm 90:12

THE YEARS OF OUR LIFE ARE SEVENTY, OR EVEN BY REASON OF STRENGTH
EIGHTY; YET THEIR SPAN IS BUT TOIL AND TROUBLE; THEY ARE SOON GONE,
AND WE FLY AWAY. —*Psalm 90:10*

THE BREVITY OF LIFE

We hear science is extending life. It is true that in prosperous countries, people live longer, but consider what the psalmist says here: Life's span is 80 years if we are strong. Yet this psalm was written 3000 years ago. No matter what age we live in, the age we live to is short.

See also: Isaiah 40:6–8

SO TEACH US TO NUMBER OUR DAYS THAT WE MAY GET A HEART OF WISDOM. —*Psalm 90:12*

A HEART OF WISDOM

We hear about people who squander money, but what about those who waste time as if they have all the time in the world. Gold is precious because the supply is finite. Time has limits as well: "Go to the ant, O sluggard; consider her ways, and be wise."

HE WHO DWELLS IN THE SHELTER OF THE MOST HIGH WILL ABIDE IN THE SHADOW OF THE ALMIGHTY. I WILL SAY TO THE LORD, "MY REFUGE AND MY FORTRESS, MY GOD, IN WHOM I TRUST." —*Psalm 91:1–2*

MY GOD, IN WHOM I TRUST

Life without Jesus is like taking a long trip without a map. I lived that way for a long time where circumstance seemed to determine direction, but in time, instead of finding a refuge from the storm, I was unwittingly traveling full steam ahead into the heart of turmoil and danger.

See also: Matthew 8:23–27

A THOUSAND MAY FALL AT YOUR SIDE, TEN THOUSAND AT YOUR RIGHT HAND, BUT IT WILL NOT COME NEAR YOU. —*Psalm 91:7*

GOD, MY REFUGE

When we see that we are living at odds with God's will for us, our choice is to enter into obedience to God's will or not. In Gethsemane, Jesus models the choice: "My Father, if it is possible, let this cup pass from me; nevertheless, not as I will, but as you will."

See also: Matthew 26:39

FOR HE WILL COMMAND HIS ANGELS CONCERNING YOU TO GUARD YOU IN ALL YOUR WAYS. ON THEIR HANDS THEY WILL BEAR YOU UP, LEST YOU STRIKE YOUR FOOT AGAINST A STONE. —*Psalm 91:11–12*

ANGELS WILL GUARD YOU

Satan distorts these words to tempt Jesus into "proving" he is the Son of God. But God knows who the righteous are. Satan's power lies in his ability to deceive the unwary; God's power rests in his desire to protect and save those who have made the Lord their dwelling place.

See also: Luke 4:9–13

"BECAUSE HE HOLDS FAST TO ME IN LOVE, I WILL DELIVER HIM; I WILL PROTECT HIM, BECAUSE HE KNOWS MY NAME." —*Psalm 91:14*

"I WILL PROTECT YOU"

Throughout history, including the present period, war, famine, and disease have been an underlying reality for most of the inhabitants of the earth. But for many of us living in prosperous lands, the darker realities have receded and with it a sense of the need for God's protection.

WHEN HE CALLS TO ME, I WILL ANSWER HIM; I WILL BE WITH HIM IN
TROUBLE; I WILL RESCUE HIM AND HONOR HIM. —*Psalm 91:15*

"I WILL ANSWER HIM"

The Word of God indicates that God is near to all who love him and that he answers
our prayers, though sometimes not exactly as we would like. Jesus left us the greatest
gift imaginable; he left the Holy Spirit. If we accept His Holy Spirit, God cannot
possibly be far away.

See also: Acts 17:27, Jeremiah 23:23

IT IS GOOD TO GIVE THANKS TO THE LORD, TO SING PRAISES TO YOUR NAME, O MOST HIGH; TO DECLARE YOUR STEADFAST LOVE IN THE MORNING, AND YOUR FAITHFULNESS BY NIGHT, TO THE MUSIC OF THE LUTE AND THE HARP, TO THE MELODY OF THE LYRE. —*Psalm 92:1–3*

GIVE THANKS TO THE LORD

Music is a great catalyst for worship. Music lifts the heart as we give thanks to God, as we praise his name for the sweet dew of the morning and for the tranquility we desire for oncoming night. Most of all, music expresses the harmony behind creation itself.

See also: Job 38:7

MIGHTIER THAN THE THUNDERS OF MANY WATERS, MIGHTIER THAN THE WAVES OF THE SEA, THE LORD ON HIGH IS MIGHTY! —*Psalm 93:4*

THE LORD IS MIGHTY

We are deceived if we believe the mightiness of kings and princes represents true power. For kings and leaders too are mortal and their reign could vanish with a mere whisper in the night. No, gauge mightiness by the works of our creator; that and that only.

See also: 1 Kings 2:1–4

YOUR DECREES ARE VERY TRUSTWORTHY; HOLINESS BEFITS YOUR HOUSE,

O LORD, FOREVERMORE. —*Psalm 93:5*

GOD IS HOLY

If we have the desire to choose the better path, then like pilgrims seeking the good way, we need signposts. Pilgrims today, walking the Camino in Spain, have an occasional yellow arrow that points the way to the Cathedral of St James in Santiago. Without signposts, we are apt to become disoriented and lost.

See also: Ezekiel 21:19

O LORD, HOW LONG SHALL THE WICKED, HOW LONG SHALL THE WICKED EXULT? —*Psalm 94:3*

HOW LONG, O LORD

Evil has not been obliterated; it seems to migrate to opportune locations to bring about sorrow, pain, and suffering. The presence of wickedness in this world is a constant and we would be wise to call upon the Lord for help and discernment. If we do nothing, the wicked will notice.

See also: Jeremiah 13:27

HE WHO PLANTED THE EAR, DOES HE NOT HEAR? HE WHO FORMED THE EYE, DOES HE NOT SEE? HE WHO DISCIPLINES THE NATIONS, DOES HE NOT REBUKE? HE WHO TEACHES KNOWLEDGE-THE LORD-KNOWS THE THOUGHTS OF MAN, THAT THEY ARE BUT A BREATH. —*Psalm 94:9–11*

THE LORD KNOWS MY EVERY THOUGHT

It is painful to watch people avoid the hard questions of life. The psalmist asks, who created the ear to hear with or the eyes to see? Great questions and three thousand years later we are still asking. So which is better: To abide in great mystery or to pretend to have knowledge?

See also: Psalm 139:15–18

WHO RISES UP FOR ME AGAINST THE WICKED? WHO STANDS UP FOR ME AGAINST EVILDOERS? IF THE LORD HAD NOT BEEN MY HELP, MY SOUL WOULD SOON HAVE LIVED IN THE LAND OF SILENCE. —*Psalm 94:16–17*

WITHOUT THE LORD I AM LOST

If we see only in earthly dimensions, we see very little. The Syrians are swarming around Jerusalem and Elisha's servant in panic sees only doom, but the prophet prays for the servant to see fully and he "saw the mountain was full of horses and chariots of fire."

See also: 2 Kings 6:17

WHEN I THOUGHT, "MY FOOT SLIPS," YOUR STEADFAST LOVE, O LORD, HELD ME UP. WHEN THE CARES OF MY HEART ARE MANY, YOUR CONSOLATIONS CHEER MY SOUL. —*Psalm 94:18–19*

MY FOOT SLIPS

As I walked along the narrow path cut into the wall of a 1,000 foot cliff, I thought only of the danger of the sheer fall inches to my right. Generally, we assume safety in our daily living, but then the curtain of security falls away revealing what it is like to walk without God.

BUT THE LORD HAS BECOME MY STRONGHOLD, AND MY GOD THE ROCK OF MY REFUGE. —*Psalm 94:22*

GOD MY STRONGHOLD

David faced Goliath, the giant Philistine, with the power of his faith, saying, "You come to me with a sword and with a spear and with a javelin, but I come to in the name of the Lord of hosts . . . For the battle is the Lord's, and he will give you into our hands."

See also: 1 Samuel 17:45–47

OH COME, LET US SING TO THE LORD; LET US MAKE A JOYFUL NOISE TO THE ROCK OF OUR SALVATION! LET US COME INTO HIS PRESENCE WITH THANKSGIVING; LET US MAKE A JOYFUL NOISE TO HIM WITH SONGS OF PRAISE! —*Psalm 95:1–2*

LET US SING TO THE LORD

When we praise God in song, we are inviting him into our presence to share with him the joy of all the blessings of grace he has lavished upon us. We are indeed blessed and our worship and song is expressing pure gratitude at the highest pitch. *Deo Omnis Gloria.*

See also: Ephesians 1:3–10

FOR HE IS OUR GOD, AND WE ARE THE PEOPLE OF HIS PASTURE, AND THE SHEEP OF HIS HAND. —*Psalm 95:7*

FOR HE IS OUR GOD

The psalmist compares God to a shepherd and his people as the sheep of his pasture. Jesus echoes this when he says "I am the good shepherd. I know my own and my own know me, just as the Father knows me and I know the Father; and I lay down my life for the sheep."

See also: John 10: 14–15

OH SING TO THE LORD A NEW SONG; SING TO THE LORD, ALL THE EARTH!
SING TO THE LORD, BLESS HIS NAME; TELL OF HIS SALVATION FROM DAY
TO DAY. —*Psalm 96:1–2*

SING TO THE LORD A NEW SONG

When we know that God knows us, we cannot repress the joy of knowing that we
are set apart by God to live in harmony with his purpose for us. Our hearts sing for
joy in gratitude for the privilege of walking with the Lord every minute of every day
as long as we draw breath.

See also: Revelation 7:9–12

LET THE HEAVENS BE GLAD, AND LET THE EARTH REJOICE; LET THE SEA ROAR, AND ALL THAT FILLS IT; LET THE FIELD EXULT, AND EVERYTHING IN IT! THEN SHALL ALL THE TREES OF THE FOREST SING FOR JOY BEFORE THE LORD, FOR HE COMES, FOR HE COMES TO JUDGE THE EARTH. —*Psalm 96:11–13*

HE WILL JUDGE THE EARTH

The earth is in joyous celebration and so are we who believe in the wonder and harmony that permeates creation. "And we know that for those who love God all things work together for good, for those who are called according to his purpose."

See also: Romans 8:28

THE LORD REIGNS, LET THE EARTH REJOICE; LET THE MANY COASTLANDS
BE GLAD! —*Psalm 97:1*

THE LORD REIGNS

The Lord reigns but his Kingdom is still to be. So what does this mean to us? Clearly, we are called to labor in his pastures. "The harvest is plentiful, but the laborers are few; therefore pray earnestly to the Lord of the harvest to send out laborers into his harvest."

See also: Matthew 9:37

HIS LIGHTNINGS LIGHT UP THE WORLD; THE EARTH SEES AND TREMBLES. THE MOUNTAINS MELT LIKE WAX BEFORE THE LORD, BEFORE THE LORD OF ALL THE EARTH. —*Psalm 97:4–5*

GOD IS LIGHT

Light and darkness are images drawn right out of the natural world, but John gives them supernatural weight. He declares in his first letter that "God is light and in him is no darkness at all." Jesus is that light as well; the very nature of God is in him.

See also: 1 John 1:5, John 1:4

THE HEAVENS PROCLAIM HIS RIGHTEOUSNESS, AND ALL PEOPLES SEE HIS GLORY. —*Psalm 97:6*

GOD'S GLORY IS CLEAR

Paul echoes the psalmist in his letter to the Romans: "For his invisible attributes, namely, his eternal power and divine nature, have been clearly perceived, ever since the creation of the world, in the things that have been made."

See also: Romans 1:20

O YOU WHO LOVE THE LORD, HATE EVIL! HE PRESERVES THE LIVES OF HIS SAINTS; HE DELIVERS THEM FROM THE HAND OF THE WICKED. —*Psalm 97:10*

LOVE THE LORD

God does not hate you or me; he hates the sin within that separates us from him. Evil thoughts translated into evil actions separates us from God and from one another. Remember the Great Commandment to love God with everything you've got. Embrace the light; dispel the darkness.

See also: Mark 12:28–31

REJOICE IN THE LORD, O YOU RIGHTEOUS, AND GIVE THANKS TO HIS HOLY NAME! —*Psalm 97:12*

REJOICE IN THE LORD

Righteousness has nothing to do with displaying an air of superiority. Claiming you are a good person while stoking a heart of darkness is not righteousness. Look to Jesus as the model for "he made himself nothing by taking the very nature of a servant."

See also: Philippians 2:5–11

MAKE A JOYFUL NOISE TO THE LORD, ALL THE EARTH; BREAK FORTH INTO JOYOUS SONG AND SING PRAISES! —*Psalm 98:4*

SING PRAISES

The cause for joy here is that "The Lord has made known his salvation." Perhaps he is referencing back to all the miracles surrounding the great exodus from Egypt, but he may also be pointing forward to God's ultimate work of salvation in the person of His Son, Jesus Christ.

See also: Psalm 98:2

LET THE SEA ROAR, AND ALL THAT FILLS IT; THE WORLD AND THOSE WHO DWELL IN IT! LET THE RIVERS CLAP THEIR HANDS; LET THE HILLS SING FOR JOY TOGETHER BEFORE THE LORD, FOR HE COMES TO JUDGE THE EARTH.

—Psalm 98:7–9

LET THE HILLS SING FOR JOY

The "seas roar and the rivers clap their hands" in anticipation of the fulfillment of God's promise that his Kingdom will reign forever. "How great are his signs, how mighty his wonders! His kingdom is an everlasting kingdom, enduring from generation to generation."

See also: Daniel 4:3

LET THEM PRAISE YOUR GREAT AND AWESOME NAME! HOLY IS HE!

—Psalm 99:3

HOLY IS HE!

Are we aspiring to walk in the footsteps of Jesus or have we been lured away by "the cares of the world and the deceitfulness of riches and the desires for other things." One path is hard, but the other is dangerous.

See also: Mark 4:19

EXALT THE LORD OUR GOD, AND WORSHIP AT HIS HOLY MOUNTAIN; FOR THE LORD OUR GOD IS HOLY! —*Psalm 99:9*

OUR GOD IS HOLY

If we choose to attempt to live apart from God, then that decision opens the way to freely indulge our unholy proclivities. As children of Jesus Christ, we are called "not to be conformed to the passions of your former ignorance," but to be holy as Christ is holy.

See also: 1 Peter 1:14–16

MAKE A JOYFUL NOISE TO THE LORD, ALL THE EARTH! SERVE THE LORD WITH GLADNESS! COME INTO HIS PRESENCE WITH SINGING! KNOW THAT THE LORD, HE IS GOD! IT IS HE WHO MADE US, AND WE ARE HIS; WE ARE HIS PEOPLE, AND THE SHEEP OF HIS PASTURE. —*Psalm 100:1–3*

SERVE THE LORD WITH GLADNESS

It is in Jesus Christ that we find our truest identity. All other identities are local and temporal. So be reconciled to God through faith in Jesus Christ, for "in him we live and move and have our being."

See also: Acts 17:28

DO NOT HIDE YOUR FACE FROM ME IN THE DAY OF MY DISTRESS! INCLINE YOUR EAR TO ME; ANSWER ME SPEEDILY IN THE DAY WHEN I CALL!

—Psalm 102:2

DO NOT HIDE FROM ME LORD

"And they heard the sound of the Lord God walking in the garden in the cool of the day, and the man and his wife hid themselves from the presence of the Lord God..." So who is hiding from whom? Could it be that we are the ones hiding and it is God who is the one seeking?

See also: Genesis 34:8

I AM LIKE A DESERT OWL OF THE WILDERNESS, LIKE AN OWL OF THE WASTE PLACES; —*Psalm 102:6*

ANSWER ME SPEEDILY, O LORD

What a picture of desolation: "I am like a desert owl, like an owl among the ruins." He says, "For my days vanish like smoke...My heart is withered like grass." Sometimes it seems the sun will not rise. The psalmist prays for help, and in such times as this, we should too.

See also: Psalm 102:6,11

FOR THE LORD BUILDS UP ZION; HE APPEARS IN HIS GLORY; HE REGARDS THE PRAYER OF THE DESTITUTE AND DOES NOT DESPISE THEIR PRAYER.

—Psalm 102:16–17

GOD HEARS THE PRAYER OF THE NEEDY

In many elite circles the biblical narrative has been set aside. The Bible, so central to our understanding of the world we live in, is deemed non–essential, irrelevant. The lights are indeed dimming when we fail to pass on "to the generation to come" the true story.

See also: Jeremiah 23:16

"O MY GOD," I SAY, "TAKE ME NOT AWAY IN THE MIDST OF MY DAYS—YOU WHOSE YEARS ENDURE THROUGHOUT ALL GENERATIONS!" —*Psalm 102:24*

TAKE ME NOT AWAY

When our days are failing and our eyes are growing dim and we are "going to our eternal home," what is the condition of our faith? Do we cling to life in fear that only oblivion lies ahead or do we believe "the Lord is my strength" and he is my salvation?

See also: Ecclesiastes 12:5, Psalm 28:7

BLESS THE LORD, O MY SOUL, AND ALL THAT IS WITHIN ME, BLESS HIS HOLY NAME! BLESS THE LORD, O MY SOUL, AND FORGET NOT ALL HIS BENEFITS,

—*Psalm 103:1–2*

BLESS THE LORD

No matter what the situation, even if we do not have the knowledge of what is happening or why, we should bless the Lord's holy name. For as it is written, "What no eye has seen, nor ear heard, nor the heart of man imagined, what God has prepared for those who love him."

See also: 1 Corinthians 2:9

BLESS THE LORD, O MY SOUL, AND FORGET NOT ALL HIS BENEFITS, WHO

FORGIVES ALL YOUR INIQUITY, WHO HEALS ALL YOUR DISEASES,

—Psalm 103:2–3

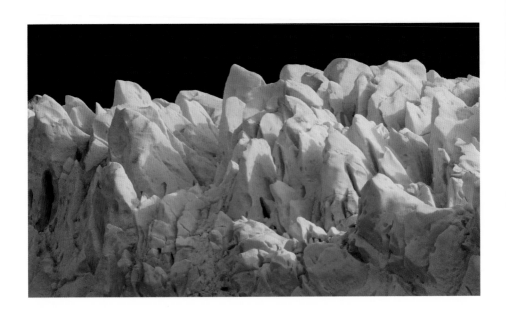

GOD FORGIVES AND HE HEALS

God blesses us through his desire and power to forgive. Unforgiven people are haunted people. Sin may begin as a tiny fleck of indiscretion, but soon enough what was small snowballs into something too heavy to bear. God can remove that weight and free us, but we must, in faith, ask.

See also: 1 John 1:9

BLESS THE LORD, O MY SOUL, AND FORGET NOT ALL HIS BENEFITS, WHO REDEEMS YOUR LIFE FROM THE PIT, WHO CROWNS YOU WITH STEADFAST LOVE AND MERCY, —*Psalm 103:2,4*

GOD LOVES YOU AND REDEEMS YOU

You have heard it said that you have been redeemed by the blood of Jesus. Think of it as a huge debt you must pay but can't. Then someone comes along who pays that debt and you are free! Wouldn't you say thank you? Wouldn't you say "thank you Jesus" for paying that debt on the cross?

See also: 2 Corinthians 5:21

BLESS THE LORD, O MY SOUL, AND FORGET NOT ALL HIS BENEFITS, WHO SATISFIES YOU WITH GOOD SO THAT YOUR YOUTH IS RENEWED LIKE THE EAGLE'S. —*Psalm 103:2,5*

GOD IS GOOD

We were born to bask in the goodness that God provides for those who love him. But isn't it true that we often ascribe abundance to the good works we have done? We are tempted to boast unabashedly about our own goodness forgetting that God is the true source, not us.

See also: Nehemiah 9:35

BLESS THE LORD, O MY SOUL, AND FORGET NOT ALL HIS BENEFITS. THE LORD WORKS RIGHTEOUSNESS AND JUSTICE FOR ALL WHO ARE OPPRESSED.

—Psalm 103:2,6

GOD IS RIGHTEOUS AND JUST

Here is a trustworthy saying: "The one who states his case first seems right, until the other comes and examines him." This verse nicely sums up the "Justice Dilemma" where human justice often mocks God with lies, deceit, greed, and many other forms of fabrication.

See also: Proverbs 18:17

BLESS THE LORD, O MY SOUL, AND FORGET NOT ALL HIS BENEFITS. HE
MADE KNOWN HIS WAYS TO MOSES, HIS ACTS TO THE PEOPLE OF ISRAEL.

—Psalm 103:2,7

GOD FREES THE PRISONER

Long after the death of Joseph, Pharaoh enslaved the Jewish people in Egypt. Then their voice rose up to God to free them from their shackles. Mankind remains imprisoned in many ways and God has responded time and again for God's desire is that we should be free.

See also: Exodus 1:1–22

BLESS THE LORD, O MY SOUL, AND FORGET NOT ALL HIS BENEFITS. THE LORD IS MERCIFUL AND GRACIOUS, SLOW TO ANGER AND ABOUNDING IN STEADFAST LOVE. —*Psalm 103:2,8*

GOD IS MERCIFUL AND GRACIOUS

If we love the Lord with all we've got and yet we stray into forbidden pastures, the Lord will always be gracious and merciful; he is a good shepherd and like the father of the prodigal son, he always longs for our return. This is why Tim Keller calls him the "Prodigal God."

See also: Luke 15:11–32

BLESS THE LORD, O MY SOUL, AND FORGET NOT ALL HIS BENEFITS. HE WILL NOT ALWAYS CHIDE, NOR WILL HE KEEP HIS ANGER FOREVER.

—Psalm 103:2,9

GOD IS SLOW TO ANGER

Cain murdered his brother, but God did not give up on him. David had his lover's husband murdered, but God forgave him. Both men suffered for their crimes, but neither lost his life. God exiled Cain but he protected him; God restored David though strife followed him.

See also: Genesis 4:11–16, Psalm 51

BLESS THE LORD, O MY SOUL, AND FORGET NOT ALL HIS BENEFITS. HE DOES NOT DEAL WITH US ACCORDING TO OUR SINS, NOR REPAY US ACCORDING TO OUR INIQUITIES. —*Psalm 103:2,10*

THE PRODIGAL GOD

"In him we have redemption through his blood, the forgiveness of our trespasses, according to the riches of his grace, which he lavished upon us...according to his purpose, which he set forth in Christ...to unite all things in him, things in heaven and things on earth."

See also: Ephesians 1:7–11

FOR AS HIGH AS THE HEAVENS ARE ABOVE THE EARTH, SO GREAT IS HIS STEADFAST LOVE TOWARD THOSE WHO FEAR HIM; AS FAR AS THE EAST IS FROM THE WEST, SO FAR DOES HE REMOVE OUR TRANSGRESSIONS FROM US.

—Psalm 103:11–13

THE LORD'S COMPASSION

Notice the qualifier: "The Lord shows compassion to those who fear him." If we turn our backs on God, if we surrender to waywardness, then what? God's love for each of us is unconditional, but we remain free to disregard him. Different consequences flow from different decisions.

See also: Genesis 4:3–7

AS FOR MAN, HIS DAYS ARE LIKE GRASS; HE FLOURISHES LIKE A FLOWER OF THE FIELD; FOR THE WIND PASSES OVER IT, AND IT IS GONE, AND ITS PLACE KNOWS IT NO MORE. —*Psalm 103:15–16*

TIME'S WINGED CHARIOT

"Man is but a breath; his days are like a passing shadow." If this is the only time we will ever have, surely then life has a tragic cast to it; death is a sleep without waking, and yet Jesus unlocks the door to this mystery of death and gives the joy of hope to all who believe.

See also: Psalm 144:4

BLESS THE LORD, O YOU HIS ANGELS, YOU MIGHTY ONES WHO DO HIS WORD, OBEYING THE VOICE OF HIS WORD! —*Psalm 103:20*

THE VOICE OF THE LORD

When God "formed your inner parts and knit you together in your mother's womb," he tuned your soul so you could hear the whispers of his soft still voice, even in the din of the noise of this clanging world. If we want to hear, we must calibrate our senses to God's sweet pitch.

See also: Psalm 139:13, 1 Kings 19:11–13

BLESS THE LORD, O MY SOUL! O LORD MY GOD, YOU ARE VERY GREAT! YOU ARE CLOTHED WITH SPLENDOR AND MAJESTY, COVERING YOURSELF WITH LIGHT AS WITH A GARMENT, STRETCHING OUT THE HEAVENS LIKE A TENT.

—Psalm 104:1–2

GOD IS VERY GREAT

All around us we see the work of art that is creation: "You make springs gush forth in the valleys; they flow between the hills; they give drink to every beast of the field; the wild donkeys quench their thirst." Yes, look and see and praise the Lord, the author of creation.

See also: Psalm 104:8–15

THE TREES OF THE LORD ARE WATERED ABUNDANTLY, THE CEDARS OF LEBANON THAT HE PLANTED. IN THEM THE BIRDS BUILD THEIR NESTS; THE STORK HAS HER HOME IN THE FIR TREES. —*Psalm 104:16–17*

THE TREES OF THE LORD

The trees of the forests are multifaceted wonders. Not only are trees beautiful to behold; they are factories of life. They produce the oxygen we breathe; they provide shade from the heat of the day, and they are the homes for birds to build nests and nurture their young.

See also: Deuteronomy 4:32–40

THE YOUNG LIONS ROAR FOR THEIR PREY, SEEKING THEIR FOOD FROM GOD.

WHEN THE SUN RISES, THEY STEAL AWAY AND LIE DOWN IN THEIR DENS.

—Psalm 104:21–22

THE YOUNG LIONS

The psalmist extols the creative, life–giving power of God. But when God withdraws, everything changes: "When you give them [food], they gather it up; when you open your hand, they are filled with good things. When you hide your face, they are dismayed" and life ebbs away.

See also: Psalm 65:11–13, Psalm 104:28–29

O LORD, HOW MANIFOLD ARE YOUR WORKS! IN WISDOM HAVE YOU MADE THEM ALL; THE EARTH IS FULL OF YOUR CREATURES. HERE IS THE SEA, GREAT AND WIDE, WHICH TEEMS WITH CREATURES INNUMERABLE, LIVING THINGS BOTH SMALL AND GREAT. —*Psalm 104:24–26*

HOW MANIFOLD ARE YOUR WORKS, O LORD

Later in the same Psalm, the psalmist breaks into praise for all the goodness of life he encounters: "I will sing to the Lord as long as I live; I will sing praise to my God while I have being."

See also: Psalm 104:33–34

MAY THE GLORY OF THE LORD ENDURE FOREVER; MAY THE LORD REJOICE IN HIS WORKS, WHO LOOKS ON THE EARTH AND IT TREMBLES, WHO TOUCHES THE MOUNTAINS AND THEY SMOKE! —*Psalm 104:31–32*

MAY GOD'S GLORY ENDURE FOREVER

The glory of creation is a shadow of heavenly things. The hand of God can be seen in the smallest details of life, but when our ancient ancestors departed paradise, sin and death marred the picture. Jesus entered this world to redeem and restore us through grace to our intended condition.

See also: Ephesians 2:4–10

GLORY IN HIS HOLY NAME; LET THE HEARTS OF THOSE WHO SEEK THE LORD REJOICE! —*Psalm 105:3*

REJOICE

God gave us a heart to glorify his Holy name, but that heart can be easily lured away by shining objects of physical adoration and beauty. Fitzgerald captures this war within the heart when Gatsby says of Daisy Buchanan, "Her voice is full of money." What does this suggest about Gatsby? About Daisy?

See also: Matthew 6:24

PRAISE THE LORD! OH GIVE THANKS TO THE LORD, FOR HE IS GOOD, FOR HIS STEADFAST LOVE ENDURES FOREVER! —*Psalm 106:1*

PRAISE THE LORD

The psalmist reminds us that all the goodness we can imagine comes from God: Righteous, abundance, life itself. But despite his goodness, we, in our blindness, have a "wanton craving" and we, like all generations before us, "put God to the test." Open the day by praising God.

See also: Matthew 4:1–11

OH GIVE THANKS TO THE LORD, FOR HE IS GOOD, FOR HIS STEADFAST LOVE
ENDURES FOREVER! —*Psalm 107:1*

GIVE THANKS TO THE LORD

God can intervene in struggles in many ways, but the ignition point is to acknowledge
your plight. This verse represents exactly what happened for me: "And call upon me
in the day of trouble; I will deliver you, and you shall honor me." I call it "God's 3
step program:" Ask, Receive, Act.

See also: Psalm 50:15

LET THEM THANK THE LORD FOR HIS STEADFAST LOVE, FOR HIS WONDROUS WORKS TO THE CHILDREN OF MAN! FOR HE SATISFIES THE LONGING SOUL, AND THE HUNGRY SOUL HE FILLS WITH GOOD THINGS. *—Psalm 107:8–9*

HE SATISFIES THE SOUL

In our busy, fretful times, filled with incoming demands for this or that, we often forget the miracle behind everything. A healthy life allows the miracles of existence to saturate our daily concerns so that we can see our story in relationship to God's story.

See also: Psalm 78: 1–11

WHOEVER IS WISE, LET HIM ATTEND TO THESE THINGS; LET THEM CONSIDER THE STEADFAST LOVE OF THE LORD. —*Psalm 107:43*

A WORD OF WISDOM

Joshua declares this to the Israelites: "Now therefore fear the Lord and serve him in sincerity and faithfulness. Put away the gods that your fathers served beyond the River . . . Choose this day whom you will serve, but as for me and my house, we will serve the Lord."

See also: Joshua 24:14–15

AWAKE, O HARP AND LYRE! I WILL AWAKE THE DAWN! I WILL GIVE THANKS TO YOU, O LORD, AMONG THE PEOPLES; I WILL SING PRAISES TO YOU AMONG THE NATIONS. FOR YOUR STEADFAST LOVE IS GREAT ABOVE THE HEAVENS; YOUR FAITHFULNESS REACHES TO THE CLOUDS. —*Psalm 108:2–4*

I WILL AWAKE THE DAWN

David's heart is filled with an overwhelming love for the Lord. And it is through the power of song that he can begin to approximate the depth and authenticity of his love for the God who has anointed and blessed him.

HELP ME, O LORD MY GOD! SAVE ME ACCORDING TO YOUR STEADFAST
LOVE! —*Psalm 109:26*

HELP ME, O LORD

David responds to God's love by singing a song that will "awaken the dawn." In another psalm, he proclaims, "For as high as the heavens are above the earth, so great is his steadfast love towards those who fear him." It is through music that David expresses the depth of this love.

See also: Isaiah 12:6

GREAT ARE THE WORKS OF THE LORD, STUDIED BY ALL WHO DELIGHT IN THEM. FULL OF SPLENDOR AND MAJESTY IS HIS WORK, AND HIS RIGHTEOUSNESS ENDURES FOREVER. —*Psalm 111:2–3*

THE WORKS OF THE LORD

"The heavens declare the glory of God. Day to day pours out speech and night to night reveals knowledge." Stephen, as he faces death, is filled with the Holy Spirit, and he "gazed into heaven and saw the glory of God, and Jesus standing at the right hand of God."

See also: Psalm 19:1, Acts 7:55

THE FEAR OF THE LORD IS THE BEGINNING OF WISDOM; ALL THOSE WHO PRACTICE IT HAVE A GOOD UNDERSTANDING. HIS PRAISE ENDURES FOREVER! —*Psalm 111:10*

THE BEGINNING OF WISDOM

After Solomon became king, he turned to God and asked to be granted wisdom to rule his people. "Give your servant an understanding mind to govern your people, that I may discern between good and evil, for who is able to govern this your great people." Wisdom starts in humility.

See also: 1 Kings 3:5–11

PRAISE THE LORD! BLESSED IS THE MAN WHO FEARS THE LORD, WHO GREATLY DELIGHTS IN HIS COMMANDMENTS! —*Psalm 112:1*

TO DELIGHT IN THE LORD

Jeremiah gives us the other side: "Cursed is the man who trusts in man and makes flesh his strength, whose heart turns away from the Lord." Solomon asked the Lord to grant him a discerning heart. This discerning heart is the seat of his wisdom; Solomon turned to God and not to himself.

See also: Jeremiah 17:5

FROM THE RISING OF THE SUN TO THE PLACE WHERE IT SETS, THE NAME OF THE LORD IS TO BE PRAISED. —*Psalm 113:3*

PRAISE THE LORD

Praising God when the sun rises and later when it sets is a fit response to the fact of creation itself. We are told that the angels sang at the dawn of creation and the psalmist echoes that when he writes, "Where morning dawns and evening fades you call forth songs of joy."

See also: Job 38:6–7, Psalm 65:8 (NIV)

NOT TO US, LORD, NOT TO US BUT TO YOUR NAME BE THE GLORY, BECAUSE OF YOUR LOVE AND FAITHFULNESS. —*Psalm 115:1*

GIVE GLORY TO GOD

"All glory to God." To say this is one thing but to live it is another. As children, many of us desired to establish our identity by winning things, but that is a child's game. When we finally figure out we are not the author of our own creation, we have taken a better path.

See also: Luke 13:22–30

I LOVE THE LORD, FOR HE HEARD MY VOICE; HE HEARD MY CRY FOR MERCY.

BECAUSE HE TURNED HIS EAR TO ME, I WILL CALL ON HIM AS LONG AS I LIVE.

—Psalm 116:1–2

I LOVE THE LORD

Where does love come from? Where did it start? John, in his first letter, clearly answers those two questions. John declares love first came from God: "We love because he first loved us." Moreover, "God is love and whoever lives in love lives in God, and God lives in him."

See also: 1 John 4:7–16

THE LORD IS GRACIOUS AND RIGHTEOUS; OUR GOD IS FULL OF COMPASSION.

—Psalm 116:5

GOD IS MERCIFUL

It would be great if we were steadfast in our mercy and love, but we often feel the impulse to strike back when we feel wronged. There is no prescription for a righteous response. We have to ingest the Jesus way. Knowing and following Jesus is "the way, the truth and the life."

See also: John 14:6

PRAISE THE LORD, ALL YOU NATIONS; EXTOL HIM, ALL YOU PEOPLES. FOR GREAT IS HIS LOVE TOWARD US, AND THE FAITHFULNESS OF THE LORD ENDURES FOREVER. PRAISE THE LORD. —*Psalm 117:1–2*

FOR ALL THINGS PRAISE THE LORD

How empty it would be if we merely mouthed the words of this psalm. The psalmist's very being is wrapped in his words. There is no space between his declaration of praise and his own life. He is saying God is everything to him. God is in him and he is pouring God's spirit out.

See also: Luke 2:25–32

GIVE THANKS TO THE LORD, FOR HE IS GOOD; HIS LOVE ENDURES FOREVER.

—*Psalm 118:1*

GOD'S LOVE ENDURES FOREVER

Isn't it wonderful to think we have a God who is patient and kind, who does not envy or boast, who is neither arrogant nor rude, nor is irritable or resentful? God is not changeable but we are, and every time we venture into darker places, we test the God who loves us.

See also: 1 Corinthians 13:1–13

WHEN HARD PRESSED, I CRIED TO THE LORD; HE BROUGHT ME INTO A SPACIOUS PLACE. THE LORD IS WITH ME; I WILL NOT BE AFRAID. WHAT CAN MERE MORTALS DO TO ME? —*Psalm 118:5–6*

WHAT CAN MAN DO TO ME?

There is plenty of evidence gleaned from the last century (and this one too) that man can bring great suffering on other human beings. When war is not raging, one senses dark forces waiting for just the right moment to cry havoc, unleashing the dogs of war in small and large ways.

See also: Genesis 65–6, Galatians 5:17–24

IT IS BETTER TO TAKE REFUGE IN THE LORD THAN TO TRUST IN HUMANS.
IT IS BETTER TO TAKE REFUGE IN THE LORD THAN TO TRUST IN PRINCES.

—*Psalm 118:8–9*

TAKE REFUGE IN THE LORD

Could it be that we elevate certain men to godlike status while dismissing God altogether? We need not look far to view the aftermath of such folly. Stalin, Hitler, and Mao may have seemed like gods to many, but they were not gods. They were killers and they killed proliferately.

See also: Exodus 20:1–11

THE LORD IS MY STRENGTH AND MY DEFENSE; HE HAS BECOME MY
SALVATION. —*Psalm 118:14*

THE LORD IS MY STRENGTH

When I was a young man, the game was to be the strongest, fastest, best player on the field. We never asked where our strength came from because we were taught, especially on the athletic fields, that our drive to win was the key. David knew the Lord, and no other, was his strength.

See also: Exodus 15:1–3

THE LORD HAS DONE IT THIS VERY DAY; LET US REJOICE TODAY AND BE GLAD.

—Psalm 118:24

THIS IS THE DAY THE LORD HAS MADE

The word "exhilaration" floods into my mind as I read David's response to the miracle of the moment when the hint of light vanquishes the remnant darkness of night. God is the artist's artist and he paints the horizon in a multitude of colors, all singing Rejoice!

See also: 2 Samuel 23:2–4

BLESSED IS HE WHO COMES IN THE NAME OF THE LORD. FROM THE HOUSE OF THE LORD WE BLESS YOU. —*Psalm 118:26*

"HOSANNA"

As Jesus enters through the gates of Jerusalem on a colt, the crowds praise him using the words of David's psalm to announce the approach of the Messiah: "Hosanna to the Son of David! Blessed is he who comes in the name of the Lord! Hosanna in the highest!"

See also: Matthew 21:9

BLESSED ARE THOSE WHOSE WAYS ARE BLAMELESS, WHO WALK ACCORDING TO THE LAW OF THE LORD. BLESSED ARE THOSE WHO KEEP HIS STATUTES AND SEEK HIM WITH ALL THEIR HEART—THEY DO NO WRONG BUT FOLLOW HIS WAYS. *—Psalm 119:1–3*

SEEK GOD WITH YOUR WHOLE HEART

It is impossible to be blameless if we do not have a relationship with God. We can play the hypocrite, displaying a handful of virtues while harboring enmity, anger, and envy deep within our hearts. But the divided heart is a killer; healing can happen through overcoming our "unbelief."

See also: 1 John 1:5–10; Mark 9:14–29

HOW CAN A YOUNG PERSON STAY ON THE PATH OF PURITY? BY LIVING ACCORDING TO YOUR WORD. I SEEK YOU WITH ALL MY HEART; DO NOT LET ME STRAY FROM YOUR COMMANDS. I HAVE HIDDEN YOUR WORD IN MY HEART THAT I MIGHT NOT SIN AGAINST YOU. —*Psalm 119:9–11*

LORD, HELP ME NOT WANDER AWAY

What will separate us from God is a heart that seeks to satisfy itself apart from God. The inclination to wander is in all of us. If we want to be right with the Lord, then we should pray for discernment; we should take each new step with care because every step counts.

See also: Hebrews 2:1–4

I HOLD FAST TO YOUR STATUTES, LORD; DO NOT LET ME BE PUT TO SHAME.

—*Psalm 119:31*

I CLING TO GOD'S WORD

Generally, our smartphones deal in information, not wisdom. Wisdom comes from God, not Google. What can we know as we wander through a maze of disconnected data? How does that leave time to "cling to the testimonies" of God? Is this really progress or something else?

See also: 2 Timothy 4:3–4

TURN MY HEART TOWARD YOUR STATUTES AND NOT TOWARD SELFISH GAIN. —*Psalm 119:36*

INCLINE MY HEART TO YOU, LORD

Our hearts are inclined to many things that can separate us from the Lord. A desire for money can replace our passion for Christ Jesus, and while we may be content in our pursuit of riches, a subtle gnawing tells us that something more valuable than money has been cast aside.

See also: Matthew 6:19–24

MAY YOUR UNFAILING LOVE COME TO ME, LORD, YOUR SALVATION, ACCORDING TO YOUR PROMISE; THEN I CAN ANSWER ANYONE WHO TAUNTS ME, FOR I TRUST IN YOUR WORD. —*Psalm 119:41–42*

I WILL HAVE AN ANSWER

Trust in God's word does not remove the difficult challenges of living in the world, but it does, when fully understood, permit us to see the truth of the nature of things from within God's towering narrative of salvation and restoration.

See also: Psalm 55:16

REMEMBER YOUR WORD TO YOUR SERVANT, FOR YOU HAVE GIVEN ME HOPE. MY COMFORT IN MY SUFFERING IS THIS: YOUR PROMISE PRESERVES MY LIFE. —*Psalm 119:49–50*

YOUR PROMISE GIVES ME LIFE

There comes a time when our sense of well-being is compromised by an affliction or loss. We remember how good it was to be dependent on our parents who loved and protected us. We want to recover that comfort and the psalmist says: trust in God. That is the way, the only way.

See also: Genesis 22:1–19

YOUR HANDS MADE ME AND FORMED ME; GIVE ME UNDERSTANDING TO LEARN YOUR COMMANDS. —*Psalm 119:73*

YOU KNOW ME

In another psalm, David says you are the God who created me and who knows my every thought: "you knitted me together in my mother's womb. I praise you, for I am fearfully and wonderfully made. Wonderful are your works; my soul knows it very well."

See also: Psalm 139:13–14

MAY YOUR UNFAILING LOVE BE MY COMFORT, ACCORDING TO YOUR PROMISE TO YOUR SERVANT. —*Psalm 119:76*

COMFORT ME, LORD

Love songs are often about betrayal and sorrow. This is because we know from experience that many of us have a hard time living faithful lives. God is different. God's love for us in unwavering. God is steadfast; he is the model and the way, even in an unsteady world.

See also: 1 John 4:19

LET YOUR COMPASSION COME TO ME THAT I MAY LIVE, FOR YOUR LAW IS
MY DELIGHT. —*Psalm 119:77*

YOUR LAW IS MY DELIGHT

We may choose to define the law as a series of prohibitions and it can be that if we permit ourselves to disregard legal boundaries. But God's law is designed with love in mind. He wants us to stay in step with him by living the Great Commandment day by day.

See also: Mark 12:28–34

ALL YOUR COMMANDS ARE TRUSTWORTHY; HELP ME, FOR I AM BEING PERSECUTED WITHOUT CAUSE. THEY ALMOST WIPED ME FROM THE EARTH, BUT I HAVE NOT FORSAKEN YOUR PRECEPTS. —*Psalm 119:86–87*

HELP ME, LORD

Technology has brought us a deluge of information that may overwhelm the ability to discern, making historical perspective a pinprick in the instant news cycle. It is unclear whether truth or lies wash down the drain first. Are we any wiser living in this deluge of data?

See also: Proverbs 1:1–7

IN YOUR UNFAILING LOVE PRESERVE MY LIFE, THAT I MAY OBEY THE STATUTES OF YOUR MOUTH. —*Psalm 119:88*

MAY I KEEP YOUR TESTIMONIES

The psalmist's sole purpose is to serve the Lord: "In the midst of the congregation I will praise you." He is not asking for long life for long life's sake. He asking God, if it is God's will, to serve His purpose while he still has the strength to do His will.

YOUR WORD, LORD, IS ETERNAL; IT STANDS FIRM IN THE HEAVENS. YOUR FAITHFULNESS CONTINUES THROUGH ALL GENERATIONS; YOU ESTABLISHED THE EARTH, AND IT ENDURES. —*Psalm 119:89–90*

YOUR WORD, LORD, IS FIRMLY FIXED

Time and again, we learn that a prophet receives God's Word through the power of the Holy Spirit. Without the Holy Spirit we cannot hear what God is saying to us. The Holy Spirit is available by the grace of God. Without it, we are deaf to God speaking to us and guiding us.

See also: Luke 14:35–36

OH, HOW I LOVE YOUR LAW! I MEDITATE ON IT ALL DAY LONG. YOUR COMMANDS ARE ALWAYS WITH ME AND MAKE ME WISER THAN MY ENEMIES.

—Psalm 119:97–98

I LOVE YOUR LAW, O LORD

The commandment of God makes the writer "wiser." In another psalm, it says "The fool says in his heart there is no God." In our own times, philosophies have been dreamt up around the idea of the perfection of man and the absence of God, creating a recipe for confusion and disaster.

See also: Psalm 14:1–3

HOW SWEET ARE YOUR WORDS TO MY TASTE, SWEETER THAN HONEY TO MY MOUTH! —*Psalm 119:103*

SWEET AS HONEY

On a walk, I passed a cluster of small yellow flowers. The bees were out in force gathering the pollen to take back to their hives where the sweet nourishing honey is made. How can it be that tiny bees can create so much good? Herein lies one of the wonders of creation itself.

See also: James 5:7, Genesis 1:2

YOUR WORD IS A LAMP FOR MY FEET, A LIGHT ON MY PATH. —*Psalm 119:105*

GOD'S WORD IS LIGHT

God's first declaration is "Let there be light." Of Jesus, John says, "The true light which gives light to everyone, was coming into the world." And in his letter John says, "God is light...and if we walk in the light...we will have fellowship with one another" and with the Son.

See also: Genesis 1:3, John 1:1–9, 1 John 1:5–7

THE UNFOLDING OF YOUR WORDS GIVES LIGHT; IT GIVES UNDERSTANDING TO THE SIMPLE. I OPEN MY MOUTH AND PANT, LONGING FOR YOUR COMMANDS. TURN TO ME AND HAVE MERCY ON ME, AS YOU ALWAYS DO TO THOSE WHO LOVE YOUR NAME. —*Psalm 119:130–132*

GOD'S WAY

"The sun will no more be your light by day, nor will the brightness of the moon shine on you, for the Lord will be your everlasting light, and your God will be your glory."

See also: Isaiah 60:19

TROUBLE AND DISTRESS HAVE COME UPON ME, BUT YOUR COMMANDS GIVE ME DELIGHT. YOUR STATUTES ARE ALWAYS RIGHTEOUS; GIVE ME UNDERSTANDING THAT I MAY LIVE. —*Psalm 119:143–144*

GIVE ME UNDERSTANDING

Give me understanding that you, Lord, are at the center of my existence. Give me understanding that without your Word I understand nothing. Give me understanding that you have set me in this place to serve you in ways that are both easy and hard.

See also: Romans 8:28

I RISE BEFORE DAWN AND CRY FOR HELP; I HAVE PUT MY HOPE IN YOUR WORD. MY EYES STAY OPEN THROUGH THE WATCHES OF THE NIGHT, THAT I MAY MEDITATE ON YOUR PROMISES. HEAR MY VOICE IN ACCORDANCE WITH YOUR LOVE; PRESERVE MY LIFE, LORD, ACCORDING TO YOUR LAWS. —*Psalm 119:147–149*

I CRY FOR HELP

My journey began as a cry to God for help. When all the promises of technology, wealth, and well–being have evaporated and we have been stripped of our pseudo–armor of position and power, what do we have left if we do not have God to call on? Sadly we have nothing, nothing at all.

    See also: Psalm 1:5-6, 1 John 3:4-7

ALL YOUR WORDS ARE TRUE; ALL YOUR RIGHTEOUS LAWS ARE ETERNAL.

—Psalm 119:160

YOUR WORD IS TRUTH

Lest we believe relativism is new, listen to the words of Pontius Pilate as he stands before the Son of God. He asks, "What is truth?" as he navigates between justice and injustice. Truth stands before him in the person of Jesus, but political forces lead Pilate to abandon truth.

See also: Psalm 1:5-6, 1 John 3:4-7

MAY MY TONGUE SING OF YOUR WORD, FOR ALL YOUR COMMANDS ARE RIGHTEOUS. —*Psalm 119:172*

YOUR COMMANDMENTS ARE RIGHT

If we live apart from God's commandments, we have chosen to live under the yoke of Satan's insidious whispers, leading us away from God. "You, my brothers and sisters, were called to be free. But do not use your freedom to indulge the flesh; rather serve one another in love."

See also: Galatians 5:13

I CALL ON THE LORD IN MY DISTRESS, AND HE ANSWERS ME. SAVE ME, LORD, FROM LYING LIPS AND FROM DECEITFUL TONGUES. —*Psalm 120:1–2*

DELIVER ME, LORD

Have the comforts of life immunized us from an awareness of dangers large and small? For those oblivious of consequences, decisions are made impulsively without regard to what might come next. Even Jerusalem lost its way, "she who was great among the nations! She has become a slave."

See also: Lamentations 1:1

I LIFT UP MY EYES TO THE MOUNTAINS—WHERE DOES MY HELP COME FROM?

MY HELP COMES FROM THE LORD, THE MAKER OF HEAVEN AND EARTH.

—Psalm 121:1–2

MY HELP COMES FROM THE LORD

When I stand on a beach and look out to sea, I think of eternity, but when my eyes see mountain peaks surrounded by islands of clouds, my mind turns to the power and majesty of our "Sovereign Lord, who made the heaven and the earth and the sea and everything in them."

See also: Acts 4:24

THE LORD WILL KEEP YOU FROM ALL HARM—HE WILL WATCH OVER YOUR LIFE; THE LORD WILL WATCH OVER YOUR COMING AND GOING BOTH NOW AND FOREVERMORE. *—Psalm 121:7–8*

THE LORD WILL PROTECT YOU

In the same Psalm, we encounter this declaration: "The Lord is your keeper." David says in another Psalm that "The Lord is my rock and my fortress and my deliverer." Accepting the truth that we are vulnerable and need a savior is a huge leap for many, but is there any other way?

See also: Psalm 18:2

PRAY FOR THE PEACE OF JERUSALEM: "MAY THOSE WHO LOVE YOU BE SECURE. MAY THERE BE PEACE WITHIN YOUR WALLS AND SECURITY WITHIN YOUR CITADELS." —*Psalm 122:6–7*

SECURITY IS WITH THE LORD

David prays for peace within the walls of Jerusalem, but peace is not a given. Elsewhere, David describes a city at war with itself: "for I see violence and strife in the city. Day and night they go around it on its walls, and iniquity and trouble are within it."

See also: Psalm 55:9–10

HAVE MERCY ON US, LORD, HAVE MERCY ON US, FOR WE HAVE ENDURED NO END OF CONTEMPT. —*Psalm 123:3*

HAVE MERCY, O LORD

For 40 years the people of Israel wandered in a "trackless waste." The people had rejected God and so they sojourned in the darkness of faithlessness and not in the light that comes through faith. Faith is the necessary link to the God that brings us to the place we are meant to be.

See also: Exodus 32:7–20

OUR HELP IS IN THE NAME OF THE LORD, THE MAKER OF HEAVEN AND EARTH. —*Psalm 124:8*

GOD IS OUR HELP

Who is afraid when walking on flat ground? But descend a trail cut into a cliff with exposure inches away and you realize that even walking can be dangerous. It is God's generous provision that sustains us even when we sense our feet are slipping with danger lurking on every side.

See also: Psalm 91:5–12

RESTORE OUR FORTUNES, LORD, LIKE STREAMS IN THE NEGEV. THOSE WHO SOW WITH TEARS WILL REAP WITH SONGS OF JOY. THOSE WHO GO OUT WEEPING, CARRYING SEED TO SOW, WILL RETURN WITH SONGS OF JOY, CARRYING SHEAVES WITH THEM. *—Psalm 126:4–6*

RESTORE US, O LORD

By asking God to "Restore our fortunes," the psalmist does not mean wealth in the usual way. He is pointing to the graciousness of God; the Lord has invited his people back into relationship with Him and so they are rejoicing. "The Lord has done great things for us."

See also: Psalm 126:1–3

UNLESS THE LORD BUILDS THE HOUSE, THE BUILDERS LABOR IN VAIN. UNLESS THE LORD WATCHES OVER THE CITY, THE GUARDS STAND WATCH IN VAIN. —*Psalm 127:1*

THE LORD IS OUR WATCHMAN

All the watchmen in the world could not have prevented Sodom from destruction once the Lord determined the people there would not turn away from the deepest depths of their depravity. Fire rained down on Sodom with its people and the city was destroyed.

See also: Jeremiah 6:17

BLESSED ARE ALL WHO FEAR THE LORD, WHO WALK IN OBEDIENCE TO HIM.

YOU WILL EAT THE FRUIT OF YOUR LABOR; —*Psalm 128:1–2*

THE FEAR OF THE LORD

Walking in the way of the Lord has eternal implications. When I was young, it was about enforced obedience, but when I found myself in a rotten place and my cry for help was answered, I finally discovered that walking in the way of the Lord brings a new understanding of freedom.

See also: Romans 8:1–2

OUT OF THE DEPTHS I CRY TO YOU, LORD; LORD, HEAR MY VOICE. LET YOUR
EARS BE ATTENTIVE TO MY CRY FOR MERCY. —*Psalm 130:1–2*

LORD, HEAR MY VOICE

There are many reasons for crying out to the Lord: We live in gratitude for all the
blessings of this life. We are lost and cannot find our way back to safety. We are in
a desperate place and are powerless to save ourselves. I have cried out to the Lord
for all these reasons.

See also: Matthew 26:36–46

I WAIT FOR THE LORD, MY WHOLE BEING WAITS, AND IN HIS WORD I PUT MY HOPE. I WAIT FOR THE LORD MORE THAN WATCHMEN WAIT FOR THE MORNING, MORE THAN WATCHMEN WAIT FOR THE MORNING. —*Psalm 130:5–6*

MY SOUL WAITS

Anticipation. We wait in expectation for our moment when all will be revealed, but without the Holy Spirit, we wait in vain for we are listening to the whispers of the world and not the Lord. In John's Gospel it says, "his time had not yet come." But when it did come, Jesus knew.

See also: John 2:1–5

ISRAEL, PUT YOUR HOPE IN THE LORD BOTH NOW AND FOREVERMORE.

—Psalm 131:3

PUT YOUR HOPE IN THE LORD

The psalmist asks, "Why, my soul are you downcast?" Elsewhere he declares, "I thirst for you...in a dry and parched land where there is no water." Deep within our souls we long for relationship, especially with God. Put your hope in him and he will satisfy that thirst.

See also: Psalm 42:5, Psalm 63:1

THE LORD SWORE AN OATH TO DAVID, A SURE OATH HE WILL NOT REVOKE:

"ONE OF YOUR OWN DESCENDANTS I WILL PLACE ON YOUR THRONE."

—Psalm 132:11

GOD'S PROMISE

David is the improbable king, the eighth son of Jesse, a mere boy, a shepherd from Bethlehem, anointed by Samuel who could not believe this boy was the chosen one of God. It would be a thousand years before the promise of God was fulfilled with Jesus' birth, the unlikely Messiah.

See also: Psalm 89:3–4

HOW GOOD AND PLEASANT IT IS WHEN GOD'S PEOPLE LIVE TOGETHER IN UNITY! IT IS LIKE PRECIOUS OIL POURED ON THE HEAD, RUNNING DOWN ON THE BEARD, RUNNING DOWN ON AARON'S BEARD, DOWN ON THE COLLAR OF HIS ROBE. —*Psalm 133:1–2*

BROTHERS

How destructive it is when enmity divides brothers. Cain turns on Abel and he kills him. Though Cain is not required to forfeit his own life, he is "sentenced" to a life of exile. He is filled with guilt, loneliness, and fear. Worse, he has lost his friendship with God.

See also: Genesis 4:1–16

PRAISE THE LORD, ALL YOU SERVANTS OF THE LORD WHO MINISTER BY NIGHT IN THE HOUSE OF THE LORD. LIFT UP YOUR HANDS IN THE SANCTUARY AND PRAISE THE LORD. —*Psalm 134:1–2*

COME, BLESS THE LORD

A pastor I admire always says "Bless the Lord" when faced with a compliment for a good sermon or a good work. He is praising God because he knows the words in the sermon and the impulse behind every good action comes through the power of the Holy Spirit dwelling within.

See also: 2 Timothy 1:14

THE IDOLS OF THE NATIONS ARE SILVER AND GOLD, MADE BY HUMAN HANDS. THEY HAVE MOUTHS, BUT CANNOT SPEAK, EYES, BUT CANNOT SEE. THEY HAVE EARS, BUT CANNOT HEAR..... THOSE WHO MAKE THEM WILL BE LIKE THEM, AND SO WILL ALL WHO TRUST IN THEM. —*Psalm 135:15–18*

TRUST NOT IN IDOLS

Since we are designed by God to worship, waves of trouble inevitably begin to pour in once we cut the cords with God and begin worshipping something other than Him. And if we do worship other gods, we will wander without a Shepherd. Inevitably, we become like lost sheep.

See also: Zechariah 10:2

GIVE THANKS TO THE LORD, FOR HE IS GOOD. HIS LOVE ENDURES FOREVER.

—Psalm 136:1

GOD'S LOVE ENDURES FOREVER

If we feel trapped in our own reality, how do we break into the truth of God's epic narrative of creation, of man, of the loss of paradise, of the wandering on the earth, redemption and restoration? For me the process began with the realization that I am in the story, just not the star.

See also: Revelation 1:1–3

GIVE THANKS TO THE LORD OF LORDS WHO ALONE DOES GREAT WONDERS, HIS LOVE ENDURES FOREVER. —*Psalm 136:3–4*

GREAT WONDERS

If life is being lived at warp speed, it may be that our line of vision is blurred, making it impossible to see the small wonders existing all around us. Panoramas are fine, but the finer details may be at our feet. God's great wonders are everywhere, both small wonders and large.

See also: Isaiah 29:13–19

GIVE THANKS TO THE LORD OF LORDS WHO BY HIS UNDERSTANDING MADE THE HEAVENS, HIS LOVE ENDURES FOREVER. —*Psalm 136:3,5*

HE MADE THE HEAVENS

It is God "who, by his power, made the earth, who established the world by his wisdom, and by his understanding stretched out the heavens."

See also: Jeremiah 10:1–14

GIVE THANKS TO THE LORD OF LORDS WHO SPREAD OUT THE EARTH
ABOVE THE WATERS, FOR HIS STEADFAST LOVE ENDURES FOREVER

—Psalm 136:3,6

HE MADE THE EARTH

The psalmist tells us that the dry land itself with its mountains, rivers, and vast plains emerged from the seas. In Genesis, the waters came first then the land: "And God said, 'Let the waters under the heavens be gathered together into one place, and let the dry land appear.'"

See also: Genesis 1:9

GIVE THANKS TO THE LORD OF LORDS WHO MADE THE GREAT LIGHTS, THE SUN TO GOVERN THE DAY, THE MOON AND STARS TO GOVERN THE NIGHT; HIS LOVE ENDURES FOREVER. —*Psalm 136:3,7–9*

HE MADE THE SUN AND THE MOON

"And God made the two great lights—the greater to rule the day and the lesser light to rule the night—and the stars. And God set them in the expanse of the heavens to give light on the earth, to rule over the day and to rule over the night."

See also: Genesis 1:16–17

GIVE THANKS TO THE LORD OF LORDS WHO DIVIDED THE RED SEA ASUNDER, HIS LOVE ENDURES FOREVER. —*Psalm 136:3,13*

HE DIVIDED THE RED SEA

Moses led his people out of slavery, but he was also leading them to the promise of the cross. The people were freed from physical slavery when God released them through the waters of the Red Sea. The waters "washed" the people but the promise of God-anointed freedom lay ahead.

See also: Hebrews 12:1–2

GIVE THANKS TO THE LORD OF LORDS WHO BROUGHT ISRAEL THROUGH THE MIDST OF (THE RED SEA), BUT OVERTHREW PHARAOH AND HIS HOST IN THE (MIDST OF IT). —*Psalm 136:3,14–15*

HE ALLOWED ISRAEL TO ESCAPE

Thanksgiving is raised as much for the consequences of the miracles of God as for the miracles themselves. Over twenty-six hundred years would pass between the exodus from Egypt to the birth of the Savior of all mankind in a small town on the outskirts of Jerusalem in the promised land.

See also: Matthew 1:18–25

GIVE THANKS TO THE LORD OF LORDS WHO LED HIS PEOPLE THROUGH THE WILDERNESS; HIS LOVE ENDURES FOREVER. —*Psalm 136:3,16*

IN THE WILDERNESS

Give thanks to the Lord for the miraculous balance that underscores every detail of His design. We live in comfort when the temperature floats between 60F and 80F degrees. Let the temperature rise higher or fall lower and it will feel like we are entering the equivalent of a wilderness experience.

See also: Matthew 8:23–27

GIVE THANKS TO THE LORD OF LORDS WHO GAVE THEIR LAND AS A HERITAGE, A HERITAGE TO ISRAEL HIS SERVANT FOR HIS STEADFAST LOVE ENDURES FOREVER. —*Psalm 136:3,21–22*

HE GAVE THE LAND

Not only did God release the Israelites from slavery, but he also promised he would lead them to a land of "milk and honey" where the people could establish a home for themselves. And even as they wandered in desert wastes, God's greater intention was continuously being worked out.

See also: Exodus 3:17

GIVE THANKS TO THE GOD OF HEAVEN. HIS LOVE ENDURES FOREVER.

—Psalm 136:26

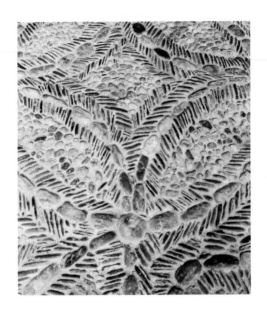

GIVE THANKS TO GOD

God's love for us begins with the creation of the man, Adam and the woman, Eve. Despite their betrayal of the One who loves them, God remains steadfast through the wreckage of human history. When we trace the biblical story, we see God's hand at work pointing to and beyond the Cross.

See also: Luke 24: 13–35

BY THE RIVERS OF BABYLON WE SAT AND WEPT WHEN WE REMEMBERED ZION. —*Psalm 137:1*

EXILED

The musical instruments have been silenced. The singers are exiles longing to return to Zion, their land before the armies of Babylon ripped them from home and family. They live separated from everything they love and the only music they can produce is the music of a dirge.

See also: Psalm 137:1–6

WHEN I CALLED, YOU ANSWERED ME; YOU GREATLY EMBOLDENED ME.

—Psalm 138:3

YOU ANSWERED ME

Jonah is a type of Everyman. God called him to Nineveh, but he runs off in the other direction. Trying to escape, he is overcome by a fierce storm at sea. He is sinking into oblivion when he cries out to God. God answers and Jonah is saved. God has saved him for a greater purpose.

See also: Jonah 2:1–9

THOUGH I WALK IN THE MIDST OF TROUBLE, YOU PRESERVE MY LIFE.

—Psalm 138:7

YOU PRESERVE MY LIFE

We live in pampered times. Danger seems to have receded, but has it? Danger can be a ruthless army decimating defenseless populations, but it can also be subtle where only you are the seeming target. God is near; He does answer in such moments. Pray always knowing God is your strength.

See also: Ephesians 6:16–20

THE LORD WILL VINDICATE ME; YOUR LOVE, LORD, ENDURES FOREVER—DO NOT ABANDON THE WORKS OF YOUR HANDS. —*Psalm 138:8*

GOD'S PURPOSE FOR ME

At some point in our formative years, our purposes often diverge from God's purpose for us. Much of the drama of the story rests on the question of whether we will return to God's purpose or will we go another way? This often private struggle can last a lifetime.

See also: Romans 7:21–25

YOU HAVE SEARCHED ME, LORD, AND YOU KNOW ME. YOU KNOW WHEN I SIT AND WHEN I RISE; YOU PERCEIVE MY THOUGHTS FROM AFAR. —*Psalm 139:1–2*

LORD, YOU KNOW ME COMPLETELY

Adam and Eve thought they could hide from God, but they were wrong. Some of us think along the same lines as darker inclinations take root. We say, "who will know?" believing that no one can see what we are doing. Something in our heart, though, tells us that he knows every thought in our heart.

See also: Isaiah 47:10

WHERE CAN I GO FROM YOUR SPIRIT? WHERE CAN I FLEE FROM YOUR PRESENCE? IF I GO UP TO THE HEAVENS, YOU ARE THERE... IF I RISE ON THE WINGS OF THE DAWN... EVEN THERE YOUR HAND WILL GUIDE ME, YOUR RIGHT HAND WILL HOLD ME FAST. —*Psalm 139:7–10*

GOD IS SPIRIT

If we live chiefly for ourselves, over time we will accumulate heavy bundles of unresolved guilt. No matter how hard we try, we are not able to unload this burden. We turn away from God as a way to escape our fears, but trying to escape from God is fruitless. There is a better way.

See also: Jonah 1:1–17

IF I SAY, "SURELY THE DARKNESS WILL HIDE ME AND THE LIGHT BECOME NIGHT AROUND ME," EVEN THE DARKNESS WILL NOT BE DARK TO YOU; THE NIGHT WILL SHINE LIKE THE DAY, FOR DARKNESS IS AS LIGHT TO YOU.

—Psalm 139:11–12

OVERWHELMING THE DARKNESS

Our limited sight binds us to seeing what our physical senses will allow. But is this enough? When the light has vanished, we say "I can't see! I can't see!" This is never true for God. He penetrates the heart of darkness; He provides the light so we can walk in His light.

See also: Genesis 1:3–5, John 12:35, Proverbs 4:18

FOR YOU CREATED MY INMOST BEING; YOU KNIT ME TOGETHER IN MY MOTHER'S WOMB. I PRAISE YOU BECAUSE I AM FEARFULLY AND WONDERFULLY MADE; YOUR WORKS ARE WONDERFUL, I KNOW THAT FULL WELL. —*Psalm 139:13–14*

LORD, YOU MADE ME

How easy it is to take for granted the infinite complexity of the human body that God "knits together in the mother's womb." We often prefer to focus on the times when this intricate "body" does not properly function rather than marvel at the miracle that is God's creation itself.

See also: Genesis 1:26–31

SEARCH ME, GOD, AND KNOW MY HEART; TEST ME AND KNOW MY ANXIOUS THOUGHTS. SEE IF THERE IS ANY OFFENSIVE WAY IN ME, AND LEAD ME IN THE WAY EVERLASTING. —*Psalm 139:23–24*

SEARCH ME, O GOD

Yes, Lord, I pray you will "lead me in the way everlasting." And yes, I will not hide from you my secret sins; my heart is open to you, for it is by your amazing grace that I am cleansed and the path I walk is the path of salvation. There is no other way.

See also: Titus 2:11–14

RESCUE ME, LORD, FROM EVILDOERS; PROTECT ME FROM THE VIOLENT,

WHO DEVISE EVIL PLANS IN THEIR HEARTS AND STIR UP WAR EVERY DAY.

—Psalm 140:1–2

DELIVER ME, O LORD

The Apostle Paul confesses that there is a power residing within his heart that aggressively desires to separate him from the love of God. He cries out in anguish, knowing the enemy dwells within: "Who will deliver me from this body of death?" His only answer: Jesus Christ.

See also: John 7:24–25

I SAY TO THE LORD, "YOU ARE MY GOD." HEAR, LORD, MY CRY FOR MERCY. SOVEREIGN LORD, MY STRONG DELIVERER, YOU SHIELD MY HEAD IN THE DAY OF BATTLE. DO NOT GRANT THE WICKED THEIR DESIRES, LORD; DO NOT LET THEIR PLANS SUCCEED. —*Psalm 140:6–8*

YOU ARE MY GOD

To believe means to know that God is real and not some vaporous delusion harbored by weak–minded people. The psalmist knows that God can free him from the snares and venom of the attacking enemy. His strength is belief in the One who can save him. His weapon: Prayer.

See also: Luke 11:1–4

I CALL TO YOU, LORD, COME QUICKLY TO ME; HEAR ME WHEN I CALL TO YOU. MAY MY PRAYER BE SET BEFORE YOU LIKE INCENSE; MAY THE LIFTING UP OF MY HANDS BE LIKE THE EVENING SACRIFICE. —*Psalm 141:1–2*

HASTEN TO ME, O LORD

God had a plan for Jonah, but Jonah went another way. Then at a moment of crisis, Jonah cried out to the Lord: "When my life was fainting away, I remembered the Lord, and my prayer came to you." At the edge of death, Jonah turned back to God and to God's mission for him.

See also: Jonah 2:5–9

BUT MY EYES ARE FIXED ON YOU, SOVEREIGN LORD; IN YOU I TAKE REFUGE—
DO NOT GIVE ME OVER TO DEATH. *—Psalm 141:8*

LEAVE ME NOT DEFENSELESS

The world devoid of God is an empty place with trouble lurking around every corner. Elsewhere, the psalmist compares himself to "a desert owl, like an owl among the ruins." And yet if we see with the eyes of the Holy Spirit, we know "The heavens declare the glory of God."

See also: Psalm 19:1–3

I CRY ALOUD TO THE LORD; I LIFT UP MY VOICE TO THE LORD FOR MERCY.

I POUR OUT BEFORE HIM MY COMPLAINT; BEFORE HIM I TELL MY TROUBLE.

—Psalm 142:1–2

I CALL UPON THE LORD

Why are we reluctant to call out to God when troubles threaten? It could be that we fear he won't answer or maybe we fear we are unworthy? Or could it be that we shy away from God altogether because we believe that we are strong enough to handle any crisis that comes our way?

See also: Psalm 28:6–7

LORD, HEAR MY PRAYER, LISTEN TO MY CRY FOR MERCY; IN YOUR FAITHFULNESS AND RIGHTEOUSNESS COME TO MY RELIEF. —*Psalm 143:1*

HEAR MY PRAYER, O LORD

The psalmist is in extreme trouble. He says, "the enemy of his soul has crushed his life to the ground." Whether it is Moses, Job, Jonah, Esther, or many others, each turns to God as the source of their strength: "The Lord is my strength and my song, and he has become my salvation."

See also: Exodus 15:2

I REMEMBER THE DAYS OF LONG AGO; I MEDITATE ON ALL YOUR WORKS AND CONSIDER WHAT YOUR HANDS HAVE DONE. I SPREAD OUT MY HANDS TO YOU; I THIRST FOR YOU LIKE A PARCHED LAND. —*Psalm 143:5–6*

MY SOUL THIRSTS FOR YOU

We are born with a thirsty soul. Solomon writes that "God has put eternity into man's heart." Our restlessness comes from seeking to fill our souls with something, anything, but if we do not fill our souls with God's Holy Spirit, we will not quench that thirst.

See also: Ecclesiastes 3:11

LET THE MORNING BRING ME WORD OF YOUR UNFAILING LOVE, FOR I HAVE PUT MY TRUST IN YOU. SHOW ME THE WAY I SHOULD GO, FOR TO YOU I ENTRUST MY LIFE. —*Psalm 143:8*

I LIFT MY SOUL UP TO YOU, O LORD

In the same Psalm, the psalmist makes an important distinction: He is not asking to be delivered from death in order to grab a little more time. No, he wants to live to serve the Lord: "For your name's sake, O Lord, preserve my life...for I am your servant...for you are my God."

See also: 1 Timothy 4:6

LORD, WHAT ARE HUMAN BEINGS THAT YOU CARE FOR THEM, MERE MORTALS THAT YOU THINK OF THEM? THEY ARE LIKE A BREATH; THEIR DAYS ARE LIKE A FLEETING SHADOW. —*Psalm 144:3–4*

MAN IS LIKE A BREATH

Time and eternity: The psalmist says we are like a breath. But eternity suggests a different reality. Job laments, "What is man, that you make so much of him?" But later he affirms his faith: "I know my redeemer lives, and at the last he will stand upon the earth."

See also: Job 19:25–27

I WILL SING A NEW SONG TO YOU, MY GOD; ON THE TEN-STRINGED LYRE I WILL MAKE MUSIC TO YOU, TO THE ONE WHO GIVES VICTORY TO KINGS, WHO DELIVERS HIS SERVANT DAVID FROM THE DEADLY SWORD.

—Psalm 144:9–10

THE SOUNDS OF MUSIC

When Shakespeare wrote, "Here will we sit and let the sounds of music creep in our ears. Soft stillness and the night become the touches of sweet harmony," he is echoing the harmony within creation itself when "all the angels shouted for joy while the morning stars sang together."

See also: Psalm 18:4–6, Job 38:7, Ecclesiastes 3:7, The Merchant of Venice

BLESSED IS THE PEOPLE OF WHOM THIS IS TRUE; BLESSED IS THE PEOPLE WHOSE GOD IS THE LORD. —*Psalm 144:15*

BLESSED ARE THE PEOPLE

In prosperous times we are apt to confuse the blessings that flow through wealth such as houses, cars, expensive fashion, and other assorted "goods" to the blessings of the Holy Spirit that come directly from God and are not dependant upon the limitations of talent, time, and place.

See also: Romans 5:17

GREAT IS THE LORD AND MOST WORTHY OF PRAISE; HIS GREATNESS NO ONE CAN FATHOM. ONE GENERATION COMMENDS YOUR WORKS TO ANOTHER; THEY TELL OF YOUR MIGHTY ACTS. —*Psalm 145:3–4*

GREAT IS THE LORD

We may say "the Lord is great" but do we live it? Paul understood that many would oppose him, but he forged on: "When reviled, we bless; when persecuted, we endure; when slandered, we entreat. We have become, and still are, like the scum of the world, the refuse of all things."

See also: 1 Corinthians 4:11–13

THE LORD IS NEAR TO ALL WHO CALL ON HIM, TO ALL WHO CALL ON HIM IN TRUTH. —*Psalm 145:18*

THE LORD IS NEAR

Is it possible to pray when you believe God is far away? It may be very hard because you may believe you are talking to yourself. But a righteous person believes God is real, near, and available. James wrote "the prayer of a righteous person is powerful and effective."

See also: Isaiah 55:6

MY MOUTH WILL SPEAK IN PRAISE OF THE LORD. LET EVERY CREATURE PRAISE HIS HOLY NAME FOR EVER AND EVER. —*Psalm 145:21*

LET ALL BLESS HIS HOLY NAME

It's not enough to praise the Lord with our lips. If our heart is not in it, our mind will wander and our words will fall to the ground to lie there alone. God wants all of us, our heart, our mind, and our soul. Our praise should be a mirror of our integrity and our mission.

See also: Revelation 4:1–11

I WILL PRAISE THE LORD ALL MY LIFE; I WILL SING PRAISE TO MY GOD AS LONG AS I LIVE. —*Psalm 146:2*

I WILL SING PRAISES

We are on a clock and we know it. We feel a tinge of sadness when a sweet trip ends; we pause as the the sun touches the horizon, with its fading light painting the western sky before the curtain of night comes down. Yes, praise the Lord day and night; praise Him always.

See also: Psalm 65:5–8

DO NOT PUT YOUR TRUST IN PRINCES, IN HUMAN BEINGS, WHO CANNOT SAVE. —*Psalm 146:3*

TRUST NOT IN PRAISES

Even if we succeed in cloistering ourselves from the push and pull of everyday life, trust remains essential. Out of our fear, we look beyond the fragile walls of our existence and ask, "Is there anyone I can trust?" The psalmist says yes, "Blessed be the Lord."

See also: Psalm 118:6–9

THE LORD GIVES SIGHT TO THE BLIND, THE LORD LIFTS UP THOSE WHO ARE BOWED DOWN, THE LORD LOVES THE RIGHTEOUS. —*Psalm 146:8*

THE LORD LOVES THE RIGHTEOUS

Who is righteous? The psalmist says, "Blessed is the man who walks not in the counsel of the wicked. He is like a tree planted by streams of water that yields its fruit in its season, and its leaf does not wither. In all he does he prospers."

See also: Psalm 1:1–3

THE LORD WATCHES OVER THE FOREIGNER AND SUSTAINS THE FATHERLESS
AND THE WIDOW, BUT HE FRUSTRATES THE WAYS OF THE WICKED.

—Psalm 146:9

RUIN

Things brand new will one day be discardable trash; even monuments, buildings. and cities will be ruined remnants of past wealth and glory. Without God to guide us as sojourners on earth, we will remain poor subjects of relentless time. If you feel lost and afraid, call upon the Lord.

See also: Lamentations 2:8–15

PRAISE THE LORD. HOW GOOD IT IS TO SING PRAISES TO OUR GOD, HOW

PLEASANT AND FITTING TO PRAISE HIM! —*Psalm 147:1*

THE SONG OF PRAISE

Music grows naturally out of a heart at peace with God. Music is an expression of abundance and love that flows from the deep well that is the yearning human heart. We sing for joy because we have let the Holy Spirit in; we have finally experienced intimacy as God designed it.

 See also: John 15:1–17

EXTOL THE LORD, JERUSALEM; PRAISE YOUR GOD, ZION. HE STRENGTHENS THE BARS OF YOUR GATES AND BLESSES YOUR PEOPLE WITHIN YOU. HE GRANTS PEACE TO YOUR BORDERS AND SATISFIES YOU WITH THE FINEST OF WHEAT. —*Psalm 147:12–14*

GOD'S MANY BLESSINGS

Have you been to Jerusalem? Go, don't wait. This is the city "built like a city closely compacted together. That is where the tribes go up—the tribes of the Lord—to praise the name of the Lord..." It is the place of the Temple and the Cross. It is where everything changed forever.

See also: Psalm 122:3–4

HE SENDS HIS COMMAND TO THE EARTH; HIS WORD RUNS SWIFTLY. HE SPREADS THE SNOW LIKE WOOL AND SCATTERS THE FROST LIKE ASHES. HE HURLS DOWN HIS HAIL LIKE PEBBLES. WHO CAN WITHSTAND HIS ICY BLAST? —*Psalm 147:15–17*

GOD'S VISIBLE POWER

The psalmist says that this miracle of life on earth was molded by the power of the hands of God. If we cannot see God's handiwork in the mystery of the workings of the earth, sun, moon, planets, and stars, then we are consigned to live a skeletal existence stripped of wonder.

See also: Genesis 1:1–31

PRAISE THE LORD. PRAISE THE LORD FROM THE HEAVENS; PRAISE HIM IN THE HEIGHTS ABOVE. PRAISE HIM, ALL HIS ANGELS; PRAISE HIM, ALL HIS HEAVENLY HOSTS. —*Psalm 148:1–2*

PRAISE THE LORD

We can know something about ourselves by paying attention to who we choose to praise. Often we limit our praise (implied or stated) to our own accomplishments or to those we know or admire, but where does God fit in? If God is not first, then who is? If not God, who?

See also: John 1:1–5

PRAISE HIM, SUN AND MOON; PRAISE HIM, ALL YOU SHINING STARS. PRAISE HIM, YOU HIGHEST HEAVENS AND YOU WATERS ABOVE THE SKIES. LET THEM PRAISE THE NAME OF THE LORD, FOR AT HIS COMMAND THEY WERE CREATED, —*Psalm 148:3–5*

WORTHY OF PRAISE

God's majesty is evident in all of creation: The rising full moon, huge as it emerges on the far horizon, the light of the setting sun as it paints the passing clouds in shades of orange and red. "Praise him, sun and moon, praise him, all you shining stars! Praise him."

See also: Isaiah 63:7

LET THEM PRAISE THE NAME OF THE LORD, FOR HIS NAME ALONE IS
EXALTED; HIS SPLENDOR IS ABOVE THE EARTH AND THE HEAVENS.

—*Psalm 148:13*

HIS MAJESTY IS ABOVE ALL

Who is to praise the Lord? "Kings of the earth and all peoples, princes and all the
rulers of the earth! Young men and maidens together, old men and children!" All of
us, every tribe and every nation should praise the Lord.

See also: Psalm 148:11–12

PRAISE THE LORD. SING TO THE LORD A NEW SONG, HIS PRAISE IN THE ASSEMBLY OF HIS FAITHFUL PEOPLE. —*Psalm 149:1*

THE CONGREGATION OF BELIEVERS

Worship is about praising the Lord. It is time set aside to concentrate our hearts and minds on the One who gave everything that we would have access to His goodness and mercy through the power of the Holy Spirit. Our time is brief; the need is great. Can you hear the call?

See also: Matthew 9:37–38, Revelation 22:7

PRAISE THE LORD. PRAISE GOD IN HIS SANCTUARY; PRAISE HIM IN HIS MIGHTY HEAVENS. PRAISE HIM FOR HIS ACTS OF POWER; PRAISE HIM FOR HIS SURPASSING GREATNESS. —*Psalm 150:1–2*

WORTHY OF PRAISE

Jesus challenges our self–imposed limitations by asking us to see every encounter on earth from God's own perspective. We are the ones who, through fear, doubt, and unbelief, create our own boundaries and prisons. The God of creation is the God of miracles; He is the God of "mighty deeds."

See also: John 17:1–26

The Lord Is My Strength began as a modest attempt to communicate through social media, particularly Twitter and Facebook, the remarkable power, beauty and relevance of the 150 Psalms of the Bible. But soon enough it began to take on a life of its own which prompted me to transform the social media postings into the book you have in your hands. Such an undertaking enlists a world of people to take the idea and build a book. I am no exception to that rule and so with a grateful heart I want to offer my profound thanks for those below who directly and indirectly had a role in creating this approach to the Psalms. My thanks to Dr. Chuck Davis for his sharing his love of Scripture; to Alison Kampmann and her sister Suzanne Holton for their incredible help in building a presence on Twitter and Facebook; to Arthur Kampmann and Peter Kampmann for their photographic "ambulatory inclinations" that grace this book; to Leon Reid who introduced me to the title of this book; to Megan Trank who has kept things running at Beaufort Books like no one else and to the wonderful team of people who have worked together to help publish this book including Mark Karis, Karen Hughes, Pauline Neuwirth, and Sharon Castlen.

All photos, unless otherwise noted, were taken by Eric Kampmann